בס״ד

Judaism
Beyond the Surface

A Spiritual Snapshot of Jewish Religion & Culture

Isaac Pirian

Table of Contents

Introduction

- Author's Insight & Reflections -

Israel, *often referred to as the **Holy Land**, beckons millions annually, while billions more yearn to experience its spiritual allure. Despite its minuscule size compared to its hostile neighbors, Israel remains a focal point of global attention. Since its inception in 1948, it has triumphed in numerous existential wars and emerged as a global leader in various fields.*

However, the disproportionate media attention has often painted a distorted picture of Israel. The reality is starkly different; Israel is a harmonious tapestry of diverse faiths and backgrounds, where Jews, Muslims, Christians, and others coexist peacefully, all considering it the holiest place for pilgrimage.

This book aims to elevate understanding of the spiritual essence enveloping a Jew's life, offering insights into Judaism without advocating for conversion. It's a journey to illuminate the spiritual and ethical landscape shaping Jewish existence and thought processes, drawing parallels with non-Jewish counterparts.

The Book's Role in Combating Anti-Semitism

Anti-Semitism, a deep-rooted prejudice against Jews, has persisted for centuries. This book serves as a beacon of understanding, aiming to dispel myths and misconceptions about Judaism and the Jewish people. By presenting an authentic portrayal of Jewish beliefs, traditions, and history, it endeavors to replace ignorance with knowledge, prejudice with understanding.

The rise of misinformation in the digital age has exacerbated the spread of anti-Semitic sentiments. False narratives about Jews and Israel often find their way into mainstream discourse. This book, by offering comprehensive insight into Judaism, acts as an antidote to such misinformation. It provides readers with a foundation to challenge and counteract prejudiced views, fostering a culture of understanding and mutual respect.

The Proliferation of Prejudice

Anti-Semitism is symptomatic of a broader societal issue. The mechanisms that allow for the spread and acceptance of anti-Semitic views are the same that enable prejudices against other communities. When one form of prejudice is left unchecked, it creates an environment where other biases can thrive.

By addressing and countering anti-Semitism, this book not only stands up for the Jewish community but also sets a precedent for challenging other forms of prejudice. It underscores the importance of education and understanding in building bridges between communities. When individuals are equipped with knowledge and empathy, they become allies in the fight against all forms of discrimination.

A Global Implication Of Anti-Semitism

Unchecked prejudice has global repercussions. History has shown that such sentiments can lead to widespread discrimination, social unrest, and even atrocities. Moreover, in an interconnected world, biases can quickly cross borders, affecting international relations.

By promoting understanding and countering anti-Semitism, this book contributes to a global movement of tolerance and acceptance. It emphasizes the shared values that unite humanity, highlighting that more similarities bind us than differences. In doing so, it paves the way for a world where individuals are judged by their character and actions, not their religious beliefs or ethnic backgrounds.

In conclusion, this endeavor is not just a reflection on the tangible but also spiritual aspects of the Holy Land and its guardians in a journey into the origins and history of Judaism. It's an exploration of what makes the land and its people holy, unraveling the mysteries of this small yet impactful nation. By understanding each other and embracing shared values, we can contribute to a world where respect and harmony prevail over prejudice and hate.

Respectfully submitted,
Isaac Pirian.

INDEX

---

1. *https://docs.google.com/document/d/17x1IKb_9hLGbsGk74zuRnScuEX-4x3QkZPNBiS6iY3w/*

   edit#heading_43ec3e5dee6e706af7766fffea512721_h.30j0zll

2. *https://docs.google.com/document/d/17x1IKb_9hLGbsGk74zuRnScuEX-4x3QkZPNBiS6iY3w/*

   edit#heading_43ec3e5dee6e706af7766fffea512721_h.3dy6vkm

Imagination

2. The Art of Gematria – The Most Ancient Known Numbering System

3. The BASIC Human, The Fundamental Composition of Humanity

4. The HOLINESS Act of Formation of the Baby

5. What is Judaism? Who is considered A Jew?

6. The Important Role of Women in Judaism

7. The Intelligence, Highest Level of Attribute Bestowed Upon Women

b. *The Holy Land; What is HOLY Anyways?*

c. *Holy Items in Judaism: Symbols of Faith and Tradition*

d. *Unveiling the Mystique of Israel, A Tourist's Guide to the Secrets of Judaism*

e. *Places in Israel Most Fail to Visit*

1. *Honoring The Divine Wisdom & Judgement in Sacred Texts*[3]

a. *The 10 commandments: The Basic Ethics of ALL Nations*

b. *The Torah and Israel:The Pic Of 10 Commandments, A Nation of Knowledge*

c. *The 613 Commandments: Nourishing the Soul*

d. *Universal Wisdom; Torah's Teachings*

e. *Education for Generations*

f. *Journeying Through the Facets of Torah: A Humble Exploration*

---

3. *https://docs.google.com/document/d/17x1IKb_9hLGbsGk74zuRnScuEX-4x3QkZPNBiS6iY3w/ edit#heading_43ec3e5dee6e706af7766fffea512721_h.17dp8vu*

1. *Patriarchs and Matriarchs: Jewish Ancestral Heritage*[4]

a. *Patriarchs*

1. Avraham, Father of All Modern Humanity
2. The Covenant of CIRCUMCISION & Promise of the Land
3. Avraham Finding a Wife for His Beloved Son.

i. Isaac
   1. The Symbol of bravery & Heroism
   2. Isaac's Blessing Saga of Jacob & Esau

i. Jacob/Yaacov
   1. Jacob's Ladder Dream
   2. ISRAEL = Another Name of Jacob
   3. Jacobs First Love - Rachel
   4. Jacob & Joseph

i. The Deed & Promise of Promised Land to Patriarchs & Beyond

a. Matriarchs (Sarah, Rivka, Rachel, Lea)

a. The Power of Words: A Cautionary Tale

1. *Jewish Rituals & Routines: Embarking on Spiritual Practices*[5]

---

4. *https://docs.google.com/document/d/17x1IKb_9hLGbsGk74zuRnScuEX-4x3QkZPNBiS6iY3w/*

   edit#heading_43ec3e5dee6e706af7766fffea512721_h.26in1rg

5. *https://docs.google.com/document/d/17x1IKb_9hLGbsGk74zuRnScuEX-*

4x3QkZPNBiS6iY3w/

edit#heading_43ec3e5dee6e706af7766fffea512721_h.2jxsxqh

6. https://docs.google.com/document/d/17x1IKb_9hLGbsGk74zuRnScuEX-4x3QkZPNBiS6iY3w/

edit#heading_43ec3e5dee6e706af7766fffea512721_h.1y810tw

7. https://docs.google.com/document/d/17x1IKb_9hLGbsGk74zuRnScuEX-4x3QkZPNBiS6iY3w/

A Journey of Rest and Renewal[8]

a. Preparation for the Shabbat, Physical & Spiritual

b. Ladies Candle Lighting Ceremony (LCLC)

c. Secrets of Judaism for a Long-Lasting Marriage Relationships

d. Collective Night Prayers at Synagogue

e. Shalom Aleichem Pair of Shabbat Angels Escort to Our Home.

f. Eshet Chail - Let's all praise the wife/mother

g. The Special Wine Blessing - fusion of Spiritual & Physical

h. The Special Wine Blessing

i. Let's Prepare to EAT

j. Birkat HaMazon, Thanksgiving Prayer - Grace After Meal {365*3}

k. The Spiritual Significance of Shabbat

l. Havdalah: A Multisensory Journey of Spiritual Upliftment

1. *Kosher Lifestyle: Nurturing Body and Soul*[9]

a. *Kashrut - Nourishing Body, Mind, and Spirit*

b. *The Foundation of Kashrut*

c. *Mindful Consumption and Ethical Choices*

d. *The Separation of Dairy and Meat*

e. *Physical Well-being and Holistic Health*

f. *Spiritual Elevation Through Nourishment*

g. *Kashrut in Israel: A Holistic Experience*

---

edit#heading_43ec3e5dee6e706af7766fffea512721_h.1ci93xb

8. *https://docs.google.com/document/d/17x1IKb_9hLGbsGk74zuRnScuEX-4x3QkZPNBiS6iY3w/*

edit#heading_43ec3e5dee6e706af7766fffea512721_h.1ci93xb

9. *https://docs.google.com/document/d/17x1IKb_9hLGbsGk74zuRnScuEX-4x3QkZPNBiS6iY3w/*

edit#heading_43ec3e5dee6e706af7766fffea512721_h.2bn6wsx

    h. *The Culinary Tapestry of Israel: "Kibbutz Galiot Effect"*

    i. *Culinary Celebrations:*

    j. *Kashrut - Culinary Ethics and Cultural Identity; The secrets of Jewish Dietary Prohibitions.*

    k. *From Limitation to Liberation-Unveiling the Spiritual Depths of Shabbat's Prohibited*

Tasks

1. <u>*Temples & Sacred Spaces: Connecting The Earth & Heaven*</u>[10]

    a. *Mishkan & Temples, the 1st, & 2nd*

    b. *The 11 Sacred Incenses*

    c. *Synagogues as Modern Temples, Secret Sacred Role of Sanctuaries*

    d. *Holiness in Architecture, Bridging Earth to Heavens*

1. *Jewish Ethical Living & Moral Values*[11]

    a. *Seven Noah Commandments – A MUST for Everyone*

    b. *Secrets of Judaism for a Long-Lasting Marriage Relationships*

    c. *Shabbat: Judaism's Gift to the World*

---

10. *https://docs.google.com/document/d/17x1IKb_9hLGbsGk74zuRnScuEX-4x3QkZPNBiS6iY3w/edit#heading_43ec3e5dee6e706af7766fffea512721_h.ihv636*

11. *https://docs.google.com/document/d/17x1IKb_9hLGbsGk74zuRnScuEX-4x3QkZPNBiS6iY3w/edit#heading_43ec3e5dee6e706af7766fffea512721_h.41mghml*

---

12. *https://docs.google.com/document/d/17x1IKb_9hLGbsGk74zuRnScuEX-4x3QkZPNBiS6iY3w/edit#heading_43ec3e5dee6e706af7766fffea512721_h.4f1mdlm*

13. *https://docs.google.com/document/d/17x1IKb_9hLGbsGk74zuRnScuEX-4x3QkZPNBiS6iY3w/edit#heading_43ec3e5dee6e706af7766fffea512721_h.3tbugp1*

Chapter 1

Foundations of Judaism: Faith, Religion, Identity, Rituals & Traditions

Introduction-Authors Insight & Reflections

Every year millions of people visit the Holy Land, Israel from different countries across the world. Yet at the same time, BILLIONS yearn to smell the fascinating citrus smell in the air, drink the water, dip in the natural water rivers & seas, walk by the vast beautiful beaches, or just the joy of touching the HOLY LAND's Western Wall in Israel for even one minute; So that one can put a personal note between the cracks of "The Kotel" soliciting varieties of blessings from Almighty.

The ONLY place in the world called the Holy Land. Place of refuge and home land of the Jews in the world, ***THE PROMISED HOLY LAND is documented in so many portions of Torah & Other sacred documents.*** The only country that grants the citizens of the world the opportunity to live in a democratic country freely Just by the fact that the person was born to Jewish mother. Another avenue is conversion to Judaism. A convert is a person who on his own ***free will*** goes through a ***rigorousprocess of conversion*** by extended learning and observing the

Jewish laws & traditions with harsh exams that most Jews would probably fail to pass.

Let's start with some interesting ***simple statistics*** (As of 2022): Please note this data is for the Middle ***East Region only***. The demographic statistics comparison to the Worldwide percentages are so minuscule that numbers will have to be shown in statistical format (not included)

	Israel	*Arab Countries in the region=22*	*Percentage Israel Vs Arab Countries*
Population (Million)	*7*	*462*	*.015%*
Area (KM2)	*22,000*	*13,000,000*	*.0016%*

As you see, the geographic area of Israel is SO SMALL that due to lack of space on the map of the world, the country's associated name can only be written on the blue section of the Mediterranean Sea!!! In case you don't believe me, search google "Israel on map of the world" By the way, this is absolutely NOT a joke NOR funny!!!

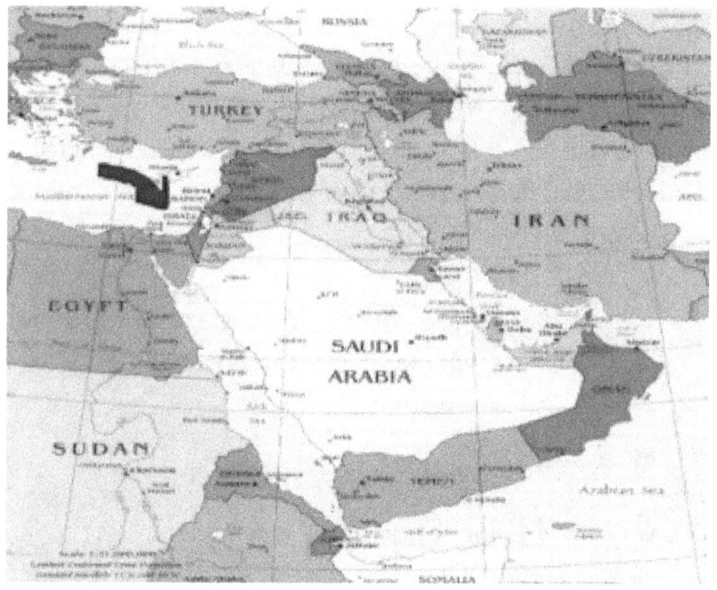

Yet, the new kid on the block ever since its inception in 1948, less than 75 years young, has faced & won number of non-initiated major wars crucial to its being & existence, whilst it has become the leading and the forefront country in the world of technology, medicine, space, science, military, &...

What is this mysterious and mystic place called Holy Land? What makes this place Holy? How did it become Holy? What is so different about this land? Can a piece of land as tangible materialistic as its sands, mountains and its water be Holy? How?

What about the people who are awarded to be as the guardian of this land, are they also Holy? What are the origins of Holiness? What are the origins of Jews? What is the history of this meager and negligible nation who is making the news so unproportionally in the world?

In the vast expanse of today's information-driven world, it's remarkable to note that Israel consistently emerges as one of the most frequently discussed countries in the realm of news and media. However, this heightened visibility also comes with its challenges, as the prevalence of fake news and misinformation has painted a totally distorted picture of Israel on the global stage. ***Regrettably, a narrative has taken hold that portrays Israel as a ruthless and unfeeling nation, where its people are constantly subjected to suppression, oppression, and silence. Yet, nothing could be further from the unvarnished truth.***

When one embarks on his fresh maiden journey to Israel, a striking and heartening realization awaits them: the authentic essence of this revered land stands in stark contrast to the misconceptions that circulate the news. Israel, often referred to as ***The Holy Land, is a vibrant tapestry where people of diverse backgrounds coexist harmoniously. Jews, Moslems, Christians, and other minority faiths such as Baha'i weave their lives together in a testament to unity with their site to this small piece of land as the Holiest place of their pilgrimage, "The Holy Land".*** This spirit of unity and coexistence is not merely a fleeting sentiment but a palpable reality that permeates daily life.Travelers are met with an atmosphere of respect, understanding, and shared humanity that defies the divisive narratives often peddled by external sources.

It's a living testament to the unwavering bonds that unite Israel's inhabitants, transcending any imposed boundaries.

Amidst the bustling streets, bustling markets, and diverse neighborhoods, it becomes evident that compassion knows no religious or cultural bounds. The friendships formed, the exchanges of warmth and kindness, and the mutual respect among neighbors from different walks of life serve as a testament to the true character of Israel.

The notion of a nation silenced or suppressed is swiftly dispelled upon witnessing the bustling cultural scene, the vibrant arts and music, the lively discussions that fill cafes, and the spirited debates that echo through the airwaves. Israelis are a people unafraid to express their opinions, to challenge the norm, and to shape their destiny. This vibrant exchange of ideas fuels a thriving democracy and embodies the essence of a society that values diverse perspectives.

In a world often dominated by polarizing narratives, Israel stands as a shining example of the extraordinary potential that can be unlocked when unity, compassion, and resilience take precedence. The real Israel is a testament to the strength of human bonds, the power of understanding, and the ability to rise above the noise of misinformation. It is a land where individuals from different walks of life coalesce, not in spite of their differences, but because of them, creating a mosaic that reflects the beauty of a shared existence.

The designation of the Jews as the "Chosen Nation" has intrigued and sparked contemplation for centuries. This distinction carries profound historical, theological, and cultural implications that have shaped the identity and endurance of the Jewish people. *The title "Chosen Nation" does not imply a sense of superiority but rather a sacred calling. It signifies a mandate to embody and exemplify the principles of justice, compassion, and ethical behavior as laid out in the Ten Commandments.*

Throughout the annals of time, the Jewish nation has navigated an astonishing tapestry of trials, tribulations, and persecutions. Remarkably, they have not only persevered but thrived, emerging as a living testament to resilience and determination. This incredible resilience is underscored by the fact that the Jewish people have outlasted numerous mighty empires, including the formidable Greek, Roman, and Persian civilizations. The question of how a relatively young and demographically small nation could repeatedly overcome such colossal forces indeed seems to transcend the realm of mere human explanation.

The essence of this enigmatic phenomenon lies in a combination of factors deeply interwoven with the essence of Jewish identity and values. One of the foundational pillars is the enduring connection to faith, tradition, and heritage. The Jews' unbreakable bond to their spiritual lineage, rooted in the teachings of the Torah and the Abrahamic covenant, has provided a wellspring of strength and unity in times of adversity. The preservation of their cultural and religious identity, even amidst persecution, has fortified the collective spirit of the Jewish people.

Furthermore, the pursuit of knowledge and education has played an integral role in the Jewish ethos. The emphasis on learning and intellectual growth has empowered the community to excel across various domains, from medicine to agriculture, and from technology to security. This dedication to continuous improvement and innovation has enabled them to not only survive but to thrive in an ever-evolving world.

The notion of being "chosen" carries with it a profound responsibility — a responsibility to embody ethical principles, social justice, and a commitment to bettering the world. This sense of purpose has propelled the Jewish people to be at the forefront of endeavors aimed at advancing humanity, contributing significantly to the progress of science, arts, and civilization.

The secret to their resilience and survival, despite the numerous challenges they have faced, lies in their capacity to adapt and evolve. This adaptability is rooted in their history of diaspora, where they have encountered diverse cultures and environments, cultivating the ability to thrive in various contexts. It is this elasticity, this willingness to embrace change while holding steadfast to core values, that has enabled the Jewish people to navigate the most trying circumstances. The modern nation of Israel, born out of a relentless pursuit of a homeland, stands as a testament to the undying spirit of the Jewish people.

The challenges they have faced and continue to confront, including regional tensions and security threats, have not deterred their determination to create a thriving and vibrant nation. Through innovation, tenacity, and a shared sense of purpose, Israel has rapidly transformed into a global powerhouse in a remarkably short span of time.

In essence, the extraordinary journey of the Jewish people exemplifies the remarkable capacity of the human spirit to transcend adversity, embrace diversity, and channel hardships into catalysts for growth and progress. The resilience, determination, and collective ethos that define the Jewish identity serve as an enduring source of inspiration not only to the Jewish community but to humanity as a whole.

To truly grasp and navigate the nuanced questions posed, it is essential to embark on a journey of understanding the foundational elements of this unique culture. At the heart of any culture lies its language, the very essence through which thoughts, ideas, and emotions find expression. The intricacies of writing, reading, comprehension, the arrangement of sentences, the significance of individual words, and the resonance of letters are all facets that illuminate the cultural tapestry.

In delving into the subject of "The Basics of Hebrew Language," we unlock the doorway to a linguistic treasure trove that has played an instrumental role in shaping the Jewish identity. This exploration encompasses the beauty of Hebrew script, its historical evolution, and the profound meanings embedded within its words. From sacred texts to modern conversations, the Hebrew language weaves together the threads of tradition, enabling a seamless bridge between generations and a deepening connection to ancient wisdom.

Within the realm of Jewish culture, an artistry known as "Gematria" takes center stage, a captivating numbering system that infuses Hebrew words and phrases with numerical values. This mystical practice is more than mere arithmetic; it is a profound method of decoding hidden meanings, uncovering connections, and revealing layers of insight. The chapter titled "The Art of Gematria, the Jewish Numbering System" navigates through the enchanting world of numerical symbolism, where letters transform into numbers and numbers resonate with spiritual significance.

As we explore these foundational aspects, we come to understand that language is not merely a medium of communication; it is a vessel that carries the collective wisdom, beliefs, and aspirations of a culture. The mastery of language opens doors to profound insights, enabling us to decipher the past, engage with the present, and envision the future.

In the forthcoming sections of this book, we shall embark on a journey that unravels the intricate layers of Jewish culture, delving into its history, traditions, philosophies, and values. With each chapter, we shall peel back the layers of time to unearth the riches of a culture that has withstood the test of time. From the ancient echoes of the patriarchs and matriarchs to the modern rhythms of a vibrant nation, we shall traverse through the annals of Jewish heritage.

Through the lens of language, tradition, and spirituality, we shall explore the profound questions that beckon us. The journey ahead is an odyssey of discovery, a quest to unravel the mysteries that have woven the tapestry of Jewish existence. As we embark on this voyage, let us not only seek answers but also cultivate a deeper appreciation for the cultural marvels that shape our world.

Strict Missionary Prohibition Laws in Judaism

At this point It is imperative for me to underscore the resolute prohibition of a Jew engaging in missionary activities or attempting to convert individuals to Judaism. The act of conversion is a deeply personal journey, one embarked upon by an individual of their own volition & will, fully comprehending the foundational principles of Judaism. This book unequivocally refrains from any form of solicitation or promotion of conversion to Judaism. Its sole purpose is to offer readers a concise and precise glimpse into the world of Jewish spirituality, a window into the intricate tapestry that envelops a Jew's daily life, religion & culture.

This undertaking does not seek to persuade or advocate for conversion; rather, it is an endeavor to illuminate and foster understanding. The objective is to shed light on the spiritual landscape that shapes a Jew's existence, to unravel the threads of their cognitive decision-making process, and to draw parallels between the thought processes of Jews and those of their non-Jewish counterparts.

It is my utter hope and aim that by reader's exposure and understanding of the characters, behavior and traits, that construct a Jew, one will challenge himself with the questions of, Why, How, Where?? While this book unfolds before your eyes an unimaginable world of wonders the next time you meet a Jew or think of Judaism and the State of Israel.

Each topic and subject explored within the confines of this document is an entry point to a vast realm of knowledge, scholarship, and interpretation of such Holy books as Torah, Gemara, Talmud, Mishna, just to name a few.

Please note the content of the book in your possession, only scratches the surface of a profound and intricate tapestry woven over centuries. Thousands of books, tracts, and commentaries stand as testament to the depth and breadth of Jewish thought, tradition, and wisdom.

This book aims to be a stepping stone, an invitation for readers to explore further, to delve into the rich fabric of Jewish culture, literature, history, and philosophy that spans millennia. It is an acknowledgement that within each brief description lies a universe of wisdom waiting to be explored, debated, and embraced.

In essence, this book serves as a compass, guiding readers through a concise yet meaningful journey into the world of Judaism. It is a testament to the intricate beauty of a tradition that has withstood the test of time and continues to illuminate the path of countless individuals seeking spiritual insight, guidance, and understanding. As readers navigate through these pages, they are invited to embark on a more profound exploration, to engage with the countless voices and perspectives that contribute to the mosaic of Jewish thought, and to discover the boundless treasures that await those who seek to understand the heart and soul of this ancient and enduring culture.

About the author, A Journey of Faith and Learning
Isaac Pirian

Born and raised in Iran, I embarked on a profound journey that traversed continents, cultures and time. With a foundation rooted in my upbringing in Iran's Shiite Muslim country. My life has been a tapestry woven with threads of Judaism, Western education, familiar with the Middle Eastern mentality and a deep faith and connection to Judaism and Israel, "The Promised Land."

The seeds of my early education were sown in the corridors of the Jewish school in Tehran, "OtzarHaTorah, Ganj Danesh" where I absorbed the laws, rituals, and values that have shaped my identity until the age of 18. Afterwards, I moved to the United States to continue my higher education. I received my Master's degree in information systems from Roosevelt University, Chicago. This transcontinental voyage broadened my perspective, combining and melding my Jewish heritage with the modern Western lifestyle.

I have been blessed with Aliah (Elevation) to Israel since 1996. Further blessed to live alongside my cherished wife, Farahnaz Bina, and our four children. My life journey has been marked by the integration of these diverse facets, blending ancient traditions with contemporary living.

In a Humble Quest for Knowledge

My voyage through life has been an exploration of faith, culture, and self-discovery. Throughout my years in the United States and, later, in Israel, I have been a passionate student of Judaism. My pursuit of knowledge has illuminated both the intricate commandments and the profound spirituality that form the core of Jewish existence.

In my quest for understanding, I have come to realize the depth and vast scope of Jewish wisdom encapsulated in the Torah, while acknowledging the limitations of my own knowledge and understanding of the Jewish laws and commandments.

A Heartfelt Gratitude

My journey has been profoundly shaped by my family, especially my wife Farahnaz Bina, who has been my guiding light and partner in upholding Jewish laws and traditions. Her role in our home is so vivid & important as her actions are spiritually elevated by the care, wisdom, intelligence (=Bina), and dedication to Patriarchs & Matriarch that she demonstrates time after time. By adhering to the observance of laws and ethics she ensures that she guides the space station of Jewish home and family life style.

This book is a testament to my humility and the recognition of my own limitations in understanding. I acknowledge that my understanding is but a minor reflection of the vast ocean of Jewish wisdom. My approach of writing is with great modesty, fully aware of the rich tapestry of scholarship woven by generations before me and the next generation.

A Glimpse into the Mysteries of Judaism

Through these pages, my uttermost intention is to offer a glimpse into the area less known and concealed from the ordinary eyes to most of humanity, with an intricate tapestry of Jewish life, spirituality, and values. I acknowledge that the subjects explored here are just fragments, drawn from the vast treasure trove of Jewish literature, including the Torah, Gemara, Talmud, Psalms, Shulchan Aruch, and various other prayer books from the *Jewish Ocean of libraries*.

In my earnest pursuit of knowledge and truth, I invite the readers to join me in this journey of exploration. I hope to provide a bridge between the profound insights of Judaism and the curiosity of the seeker, balancing intellectual rigor with approachability by providing the most of the information, with the simplest language in explaining the challenges of the complex each of the subjects discussed.

As you delve into the pages of this book, keep in mind that the subjects discussed are offered as a modest window into the expansive world of Jewish thought. My goal is to present the information as complete as possible, while explaining the subjects as clearly and concisely as possible, allowing readers to engage with these concepts with depth and clarity.

As The Journey Continues

My ongoing journey is, a perpetual quest to uncover the layers of wisdom within Judaism, has brought me to recognize that perhaps interpretation and simplification have gone awry in quest to bring the subjects to the reader as concise and as simple as possible. Perhaps striking a balance between academic rigor and accessibility. As you explore the contents of this book, consider it an invitation to dive deeper into the Ocean of Jewish knowledge, where every ripple carries the resonance of centuries of learning and reflection.

A personal note to the Holy One, G-Almighty

Where do I begin? My small brain, and human attributes do not even allow me to praise you properly as necessary. So much to say and not enough ink to write them all. I will try anyways, because that is the best I know how, as you planted it in me.

First, I would like to thank you for letting me be the person I am. Allowing me to live, with the ample and generous blessings that you have bestowed upon me. Empowered me to praise you all the time by the knowledge and understanding that you have created me and everything around me. Your bountiful wisdom, insight and foresight in caring for ALL your establishments in the world as the King of The Kings, everywhere, every time. As you even ensure and safeguard the nourishment necessary for an egg 21 days in a closed environment (no deliveries accepted☺) before the egg turns magically to a chick; For your abundance to provide for the health, well-being and sustenance of All your creations All the time and it does not stop at the story of an egg.

My generous and bountiful personal thanks to your holiness G-Almighty, for having given me the opportunity to bring this book to light with the wisdom and abilities necessary to accomplish this Holy task.

At this point I would like to bring to your Holiness my apologies and requesting forgiveness if by any ways I have overstepped my borders and boundaries by oversimplification and (G-D forbid) even to sub-level of mis-interpretation or mis-conception of the laws, while trying to present the spiritual aspect of Jewish religion and culture in an informative, interesting and challenging way to the novice reader from all corners of this World we call home.

A Humble Request for Guidance

I plead with your highness, G-Almighty, to guide me in correcting any misinterpretations or errors that I might have introduced. Your wisdom and clarity are my guiding lights, and I humbly seek your illumination to rectify any missteps and lead myself and others onto the path of truth.

My ultimate goal has been to convey to the reader a sense of your Almighty's brilliance and the splendor of your Omnipresence in every facet of our existence. May your warmth and blessings envelop the reader, their families, and all those who they hold dear. Your immense & infinite love for all your creations is evident, and I beseech you to continue showering your love upon us.

A Path Illuminated by Your Light

As I continue on this journey of sharing knowledge and insights, I pray that your divine light shines brightly upon me, guiding me along the proper trail. Your wisdom is the beacon that leads to your majestic castle, the realm of the King of Kings. With utmost sincerity and devotion, I aspire to follow this luminous path that you have graciously paved for all who seek your truth.

May your infinite compassion and understanding envelop us all, leading us to a deeper connection with your divine presence. In your benevolence, I find solace and purpose, and I am eternally grateful for the opportunity to share your light with others, with the utmost respect and humility.

An Open Heart Memo and Sincere Intentions to our Dear Reader

In the unlikely event that any aspect of the material presented within these pages has been inadvertently inaccurate or has caused any misguidance, I humbly offer my deepest apologies. My intentions have always been rooted in sincerity and a genuine desire to share insights and understanding.

If at any point, the material has fallen short of accuracy, I assure you, it has not been as a result of deliberate intention' rather, it has stemmed from the limitations of my own understanding or an oversight in comprehending the vastness of your magnificence and grandeur.

Isaac Pirian,

Almighty's 24 Hour Servant

Abbreviations

G-A: An Abbreviation for G-d Almighty. Why?

This abbreviation is not just to save on few more keystrokes, **rather, A closer look at the third commandment instructs** us not to use the name of G-d without a valid purpose, the abbreviation "G-A" is employed as a mark of reverence and respect. By refraining from fully spelling and pronouncing out the sacred name, we honor the divine commandment and preserve the sanctity of G-d's name.

This practice is in alignment with the deep-rooted tradition of not taking the name of G-d lightly or in vain. It reflects our understanding of the profound significance of the Divine and serves as a reminder of the reverence with which we approach the sacred. It further reminds us to mention G-Almighty name with reverence and awe anytime especially when not in prayer.

GENIZA: Honoring Sacred Texts: Furthermore, in accordance with the respect we hold for G-d's name and the sanctity of our sacred texts, it is imperative to treat documents containing G-d's name with the utmost care. As stated, disposal by common methods such as discarding in the trash, cutting, or shredding is not appropriate. Instead, these ***documents, including old scrolls, Torahs, Siddurim, pamphlets, or any other materials with G-d's name, must be given a proper burial ceremony= GENIZA***. This ceremony is a demonstration of the profound respect we hold for G-d's name and the teachings that it embodies.

By adhering to these practices, we not only uphold the principles of our faith but also express our unwavering commitment to preserving the sanctity of our traditions and the reverence we hold for the Divine.

The "Chosen" Nation

Embracing Responsibility and Illuminating the World with the Knowledge of the EverlastingTorah teachings

The title "Chosen Nation" was bestowed to Jews/Israelites on Mount Sinai as the people who were selected to be in covenant with G-Almighty. While members of all nations are loved, there is a special place in the heart of G-Almighty for his favorite son for accepting the 10 commandments without even knowing them in advance. Jews, while in awe of, affirmed together the call of G-Almighty "NaasehV'Nishma". We first abide by accepting the laws and only then we will listen or learn and consequently teach them.

The verse where G-Almighty bestows the title of "The Chosen Nation" to Jews: Exodus 19:5: *"Now therefore, if you will indeed obey my voice and keep my covenant, you shall be my treasured possession among all peoples, for all the earth is mine."*

Let's digest this title. The liberty to use this title is not as simple as you might think. **"Chosen Nation " It is not** *just a fancy two words Slogan title! It is only given to Jews, to be G-Almighty voice and keep the covenants as a prerequisite.*

The designation of "Chosen Nation" carries profound significance within the fabric of Jewish identity. Far from being a mere linguistic descriptor, this title encapsulates a weighty commitment, a covenant with the Divine that extends beyond personal boundaries to encompass the well-being of all humanity.

To fully grasp the implications of this title, one must delve into its intricate layers, unveiling a profound connection between chosen-ness and responsibility. At its core, being the "Chosen Nation" means embracing a dual role: an ambassador of enlightenment and a custodian of justice.

This sacred designation bestows a lofty responsibility, a duty not only to excel individually but also to uplift the collective human experience. It signifies an obligation to radiate knowledge, compassion, and morality, dispelling the shadows of ignorance, intolerance, and injustice that often shroud the world.

The notion of chosen-ness, therefore, extends beyond a self-serving privilege. It demands a dedication to the pursuit of wisdom, to the dissemination of knowledge, and to the active pursuit of justice. It is a recognition that the illumination of one's own path is intimately intertwined with the illumination of the paths of others.

Through the prism of chosen-ness, Jews are summoned to perpetuate the torch of knowledge and peace, serving as beacons of hope in a world often besieged by darkness. This mantle of responsibility requires vigilance, persistence, and an unwavering commitment to ethical conduct.

The concept of being chosen extends beyond religious rituals and transcends geopolitical boundaries. It is a clarion call to champion human dignity, compassion, and understanding. By living up to the ideals of chosen-ness, Jews become ambassadors of healing in a fractured world, catalysts for positive change, and conduits of goodwill.

This venerated title finds its roots in ancient history, echoing through the annals of time as a testament to the enduring bond between the Jewish people and the Divine. It beckons Jews to exemplify the finest qualities of humanity, empathy, integrity, and resilience, and to utilize their chosen status as a catalyst for progress.

The contemporary implications of this chosen-ness are manifold. In an era characterized by division and discord, the responsibility to foster unity, harmony, and empathy is paramount. By harnessing the power of chosen-ness, Jews possess the capacity to bridge divides, amplify understanding, and build bridges of connection.

Moreover, the mantle of chosen-ness serves as a profound reminder that with privilege comes obligation. The quest for personal growth is intricately linked to the mission of nurturing a just and compassionate society. The chosen-ness narrative compels Jews to challenge inequities, champion human rights, and work tirelessly to uplift the vulnerable and oppressed.

In the modern world, where the echoes of hatred and intolerance reverberate, the concept of chosen-ness serves as a beacon of hope and a call to action. By channeling the essence of chosen-ness into acts of kindness, charity, and advocacy, Jews can contribute to the realization of a more just, equitable, and harmonious world.

Ultimately, the title "Chosen Nation" encapsulates a profound truth: that the privilege of chosen-ness is intertwined with the imperative of responsibility. By embracing this dual role, as bearers of enlightenment and stewards of justice, Jews can fulfill their sacred mandate to illuminate the world with the transformative light of compassion, wisdom, and righteousness.

The "One" Nation

The Hebrew phrase "Am Echad" (עַם אֶחָד) translates to "One People" or "One Nation." It signifies unity and shared identity, transcending geographical borders and cultural diversities.

Up to the time prior to Exodus, the Israelites were considered Jewish, the descendants of Avraham. During the exodus, while they had camped on Mount Sinai, Moses brought the two Tablets that were etched by G-Almighty's fingers. The act of acceptance of Torah by Jewish people elevates their status to a higher spiritual level by making all Jews as The One Nation who accepted the Torah's commandments & laws.

Rooted in the opening verse of the Shema, it resonates with a resounding truth: ***"Hear, O Israel: That our God is the Omnipresence, the G-Almighty is One."***

Am Echad, by being the only Nation, who made an everlasting covenant with the ONE G-Almighty to belong to him.

The moral aspect of "Am Echad" is ingrained in the Jewish ethics and culture, emphasizing collective responsibility. It encompasses compassion, justice, and kindness. The Jewish tradition values social justice and Tikkun Olam (repairing the world), fostering moral cohesion within the community.

"Am Echad" is intertwined with the spiritual fabric of Judaism. It signifies a shared spiritual heritage that transcends individual rituals. This unity is rooted in the belief in a singular, eternal, and transcendent G-Almighty, fostering a sense of moral cohesion within the larger community.

In history, the moral and spiritual aspects of "Am Echad" prevailed among Jews, exemplifying unity and resilience. The concept's moral and spiritual underpinnings helped Jews persevere through horrifying human challenges like the Holocaust.

The concept is integral to the connection to the land of Israel, symbolizing a spiritual bond. The aspiration to return to the ancestral homeland is a manifestation of the moral and spiritual unity that "Am Echad" represents.

"Kol Yisrael Arevim Zeh Bazeh" (Every Israelites is responsible for one another) reflects collective responsibility. The value of "Ahavat Yisrael" (love for one's fellow Jews) emphasizes unity and empathy. This wonderful trait gives the responsibility to the person to feel another person, in good times or challenging times.

Spiritually, "Am Echad" is evident in communal prayers, gatherings, and festival celebrations. These actions reinforce the concept of a unified people with a common spiritual heritage.

"Am Echad" embodies the moral and spiritual core of Judaism. It signifies unity, responsibility, and shared spirituality, guiding the Jewish people throughout history. It fosters moral cohesion and emphasizes compassion and justice. Spiritually, it underscores the belief in a singular, transcendent G-A and a shared divine purpose. "Am Echad" is a source of strength in adversity and a guiding light in the Jewish pursuit of moral and spiritual excellence. Through it, the Jews embrace the collective identity, celebrating shared history, values, and destiny while promoting a just and compassionate world.

The "BOOK" Nation

Example of Daf – A page of Gemara/Talmud, 41 tracts, Total of SUCH pages: 2711

Embarking on our journey to quench the thirst for knowledge, we find ourselves drawing inspiration from the legacy of our ancestors. In our pursuit of unraveling profound questions, we inevitably turn to the beacon of wisdom that has guided humanity for ages, The Torah, the sacred scripture of the Jewish people holds the foundational text the key to understanding the origins of the Jewish faith, the iconic figures who shaped its course, and the invaluable teachings they imparted to humanity.

At the heart of this exploration lies the essential query: where did the Jewish religion find its genesis? The Torah, often referred to as the Five Books of Moses, serves as the cornerstone of Jewish theology and ethical guidance. Through its pages, we encounter a tapestry of narratives, laws, and profound wisdom that offers profound insights into the nature of human existence and our relationship with the Divine.

The journey of the Jewish people, epitomized by the exodus from Egypt, culminated in a transformative moment atop Mount Sinai. It was here that the Torah, a divine covenant between the Jewish people and their Creator, was bestowed. Within its pages lay a blueprint for righteous living, establishing a moral compass for individuals and societies alike. The Torah's commandments, numbering 613, encompass a vast array of ethical, moral, and ritual obligations that continue to shape the lives of Jews to this day.

The teachings of the Torah are encapsulated within the first five books attributed to Moses: Genesis, Exodus, Leviticus, Numbers, and Deuteronomy. These sacred texts offer insights into the creation of the world, the journey of the Israelites, the establishment of laws, and the forging of an unbreakable bond between the Jewish people and their Creator. As we delve into these narratives, we uncover the profound attributes introduced by iconic figures, from the unwavering faith of Abraham to the leadership of Moses and the resilience of the Israelites.

The principle of Jewish education extends beyond the Torah itself, embracing the wisdom of the "Nevi'im", the Prophets. These visionary individuals held direct communication with the Divine, imparting invaluable messages of hope, warning, and guidance. The era of the First Temple in Israel, spanning from Moses' passing to the Babylonian conquest, is chronicled within these texts. The Prophets offer insights into the challenges faced by the Israelites, the consequences of their actions, and the enduring promise of redemption.

Completing the triad of Jewish education is the "Ketuvim," or the Writings. This collection includes eleven diverse books, each contributing a unique perspective on wisdom, poetry, historical records, and profound reflections. Among its treasures are the poetic Psalms, the pragmatic Proverbs, the passionate Song of Songs, and the introspective Ecclesiastes. These writings, initially debated for inclusion in the Biblical canon, provide a multi-faceted view of human experience, offering solace, guidance, and an intimate connection to the Divine.

The transmission of Torah wisdom extends beyond the written word, passing from generation to generation through oral tradition. Even after the destruction of the Second Holy Temple, the commitment to learning and teaching Torah remained unwavering. The mantle of leadership was taken up by Rabbi Yehuda HaNasi, who compiled the Mishnah, a foundational work that encapsulated the Jewish oral tradition and legal discussions.

In essence, the Jewish people have embraced the mantle of being the "Nation of the Book," entrusted with safeguarding and disseminating the profound teachings of the Torah. This sacred duty encompasses not only the study of ancient texts but also the living embodiment of the values and principles they espouse. Through this sacred commitment, the Jewish people have preserved their heritage, strengthened their identity, and enriched the world with timeless wisdom.

The "Startup Nation"

The extraordinary emergence of Israel as a global hub for innovation, entrepreneurship, and technological advancement. This term encapsulates the rapid growth and success of Israel's startup ecosystem, which has garnered international attention and admiration.

The long journey of Israel from a young nation grappling with existential challenges to becoming a powerhouse of innovation is a testament to its resilience, resourcefulness, and unwavering spirit. Despite its relatively minute size, population and geopolitical complexities, Israel has managed to cultivate an environment that fosters creativity, disrupts traditional industries, and produces groundbreaking technologies day after day.

Several factors contribute to the phenomenon of Startup Nation. First and foremost is the emphasis on education and research. Israel boasts a world-class education system and a high percentage of citizens with advanced degrees in various fields. This well-educated workforce forms the foundation for the country's innovation-driven economy.

Additionally, Israel's mandatory military service plays a role in nurturing skills such as leadership, problem-solving, and adaptability. Many of these skills grasped during the Army Service are directly transferable to the startup world, where quick thinking and agile decision-making are essential.

A culture of resilience and risk-taking is another defining aspect. The Israeli society's history of facing adversity has bred a spirit of perseverance and a willingness to take on challenges. This mindset has translated into the entrepreneurial realm, where startups often tackle ambitious projects with a willingness to pivot and learn from failures.

Furthermore, government policies have played a significant role in supporting startups. Various initiatives, grants, and tax incentives have been put in place to encourage entrepreneurship and attract foreign investors. Moreover, a strong collaboration between academia, industry, and government has created a synergy that propels innovation forward.

The presence of venture capital firms and angel investors, both local and international, has provided startups with the necessary funding to transform ideas into reality. These investors are drawn to Israel's culture of innovation and its reputation for producing cutting-edge technologies.

A prime example of Startup Nation's success can be seen in Israel's leadership in sectors such as cybersecurity, artificial intelligence, biotechnology, and clean energy. Companies like Waze, Mobileye, and Iron Dome are just a few examples of Israeli innovations that have had a global impact.

In conclusion, the term "Startup Nation" encapsulates Israel's remarkable journey from a struggling nation to a global innovation powerhouse. The confluence of education, military service, culture, government support, and investment has created an ecosystem where startups thrive, disrupt industries, and contribute to shaping the future. Israel's ability to embrace challenges, pivot in the face of adversity, and harness its human capital for technological advancement is a beacon of inspiration for nations around the world.

Einstein's Quote on coexistence & cohesion of Religion & Science:
"Science without religion is lame, religion without science is blind."

This statement reflects Einstein's perspective on the relationship between science and religion and emphasizes the idea that both have their unique roles in human understanding and progress.

1. **"Science without religion is lame"**: In this part of the quote, Einstein suggests that science, which is the pursuit of knowledge through empirical observation, experimentation, and rational thinking, can be limited or "lame" without the inclusion of religious or ethical values. Science provides us with knowledge about the natural world, but it doesn't

inherently offer moral or ethical guidance. Without these guiding principles, scientific knowledge alone may not help humanity make wise decisions or lead to a meaningful existence. In other words, it implies that science should be accompanied by ethical and moral considerations for its applications to be truly beneficial.

2. **"Religion without science is blind"**: In the second part of the quote, Einstein emphasizes that religion, which often provides a moral and spiritual framework for individuals and communities, can be "blind" without an understanding of the natural world through scientific inquiry. This suggests that faith and spirituality should be informed by a broader understanding of the physical universe. Without such understanding, religious beliefs may lack a foundation in reality and may lead to dogmatism or superstition. By incorporating scientific knowledge, religion can become more grounded and adaptable to the changing world.

In essence, Einstein's quote encourages a harmonious coexistence between science and religion, where each contributes to different aspects of human existence. He believed that when science and religion complement each other, they can offer a more balanced and enlightened perspective on the complexities of the universe and our place within it. It's important to note that Einstein's views on religion were of his personal Jewish religious doctrine's spirituality and ethics upbringing.

For Einstein, a balanced perspective that integrates both scientific and spiritual insights was essential for a more complete understanding of the world and our place in it.

Chapter 2

Journeying Through Judaism BASICS

HEBREW: The Jewish Language
" Beyond Human Eyesight and Imagination "

G-Almighty embarked on the wondrous act of creation through ten

utterances, each a symphony of divine thought and word. These words

are not merely ink on paper; they are vessels of profound power,

brimming with personal significance that transcends their

transformation into words that describe the world's creation. The combination and unification of the Hebrew letters to Hebrew words by

allowing our limited and bounded mind to understand the meaning of

the words. The ten utterances of commandments used the 22 Hebrew

letters to etch the eternity for the Humanity.

Within each of the Hebrew letters lies a universe of intellectual and spiritual depth waiting to be explored. Libraries overflow with volumes dedicated to dissecting the layers of meaning within each letter, its shape & drawing, insights from Torah, Talmud, and Gemara. Yet, even in the grand fabric of scholarly exploration, the essence of G-Almighty remains elusive, a holiness beyond human comprehension.

The very shapes of the letters carry ancient wisdom, etched onto tablets by the divine fingers. Consider the profound origin of the *Hebrew alphabet, the oldest known language to humanity*. Moses carried the Torah Tablets down from the sacred mountain Sinai, their forms shaped by G-Almighty's own fingers after forty days of Moses prayers and fasting.

Each of the 22 Hebrew letters hold a unique tale that is each worth a screenplay movie by itself, a puzzle piece of cosmic significance.

Justto introduce you to the tip of the iceberg on Hebrew, I will present to you some of the intricacies and complexities of the Hebrew language on the first letter

"ALEF= אלף= א"

The letter "א" (alef) written composition is a fusion of three letters: "26= (10+6+10)" = "י" + "ו" + "י" . Confused? Here is a bit more clarification:

Let's look at the letter "א" carefully, in writing the letter start

1. The first part "י" starts from right corner diagonally towards left,

2. The 2nd letter "ד" starts from top left corner diagonally towards the bottom of the right corner

3. The last part of the letter is again "י" drawn from the middle of the diagonal of "ד" to the bottom of the left corner. You might rightfully say how is this one counted for another 10? So here is what Jewish knowledge and insight brings to the table. Look at the 3rd part just drawn; if you look at it not just what meets the eyes at first, but look at it as they say, "Outside the Box" The letter drawn is another י, only it is upside down!

Strange? Maybe. But could the drawing of the third part of the first letter א and its deep internal meaning and reasoning be the essence of the Jewish survival? By looking at the situations through unconventional methods? Looking deep into the root of the items? By accepting the fact that things are not really what they look like to be. By conforming to the logical process in everyday decisions, by taking the time to dissect them to the simpler & simpler forms in trying to solve the problems that affect him or humanity. BTW Here is a gift of Judaism to humanity; "Patience" and its importance in our daily lives and decisions.

"ELEF= אלף= א , Vocalization"

The vocalization of this first letter, brings 3 different letters to our lips and mind: Here it is a fusion of three letters:["ף" + "ל" + "א" (Alef+Lamed+Pe)]. This intricate construction impregnates another numerical value for the letter א new calculation: "(1+30+80) =111 or (1+30+800) =831."

But the letter's journey does not stop there. Its vocalization, "Alef = Elef", resonates with the potent energy value of 1000. Such revelations are but a glimpse into the marvels of Gematria, a subject so intricate and captivating that it could fill volumes of books in their own right.

Please accept this brief and modest Gematria explanation, as really the tip of the iceberg in the wonderous and mystic world of Hebrew alphabet, "Beyond Eyesight & Imagination" clarified or the still hidden and unknown.

And yet, beyond the enigma of Hebrew Gematria, lies a universe of related fields beckons such as: Punctuation, Sounds, Tags, RasheiTevot (the sequence of the letters starting in words), SofeiTevot (the sequence of the words ending letters) and clusters of letters form intricate webs of knowledge, inviting scholars to dive into their depths.

The mastery of these fields is no mere feat; it requires years of dedicated study, comparable to a four-year degree.

As our journey through the essence of Judaism unfolds, some mysteries must remain for future exploration. The multifaceted realm of letters and their interconnected meanings offers a glimpse into the boundless wisdom of G-Almighty. Our purpose here is to offer a window into this expansive realm, a glimpse into the richness that awaits those who seek to unravel its secrets.

The Art of Gematria
The most ancient known numbering system

There are 22 Hebrew letters, which G-Almighty has uttered to establish the World. These letters are considered HOLY each with its own spiritual realm. As such utmost respect & attention must be granted in their usage. It is forbidden to utter, write, or even think about the Hebrew letters in unclean places, such as the bathroom!

In addition to a letter being a **letter**, and combining with other letters make words & sentences and its specific meanings; Each letter also has a **number value** associated to them, i.e. "A=1א= , B=2=ב" & so forth. The following table presented the Hebrew letters (table below) associated values systems in the order of the 22 letters:

$(1,2,3...10,20,30,...100,200,300,400)$

Words or sentences are created by combining different letters, which means the mathematical associated numbering system will follow as well.

The letters and its numbering associations sheds light on the insight and correlation between different word or sentences who compose

50

Pronounce	Number Value	Hebrew letters
Alef	1	א
Beth	2	ב
Gimel	3	ג
Dalet	4	ד
Heh	5	ה
Vov	6	ו
Zain	7	ז
Cheth	8	ח
Teth	9	ט
Yud	10	י
Chaf	20	כ
Lamed	30	ל
Mem	40	מ
Noon	50	נ
Samech	60	ס
Aaiin	70	ע
Pe	80	פ
Zadi	90	צ
Kuf	100	ק
Resh	200	ר
Shin	300	ש
Thaf	400	ת
Chaf Sofi *	500	ך
Mem Sofi *	600	ם
Nun Sofi *	700	ן
Pe Sofi *	800	ף
Zadi Sofi *	900	ץ
Alef=Alef	1000	א

And here is another amazing fact about the letter *"Alef"*, in addition to its value of 1, it is also pronounced *"Elef* =1000". One more fact, as the cherry on top of the cake, it can also be pronounced *"Aluf "*, which means General, Master, or Champion, which is reserved for ***The one & the only***.

G-Almighty created the world by uttering the 22 words. You might have just said, "Wait, here are 28 not 22!" You are right. In the written arena of the Hebrew letters, there are 5 letters that are written differently when it falls as the last letter of the word (Sofi=End). The 5 last letters in the table above (with *) are as such. They are also referred to as "MANSPACH מנצפך" letters. 22+5=27".

As I mentioned, this book is part of my personal journey in exploring my roots in Judaism. In this quest, I can express to you my surprise to find a good portion of observing Jews or who understand the Gematria are not aware of the less known great values of these letters from 500 to 900 and I am sure they will hit the books to research the validity of my remarks on the high valued MANSPACH letters.

My search for understanding *"Why these letters are not commonly used in our daily numbering system"* has gone awry. I have heard a few reasons from older generations that could satisfy the curiosity. Although I do not have a way to confirm these hearsays. The most acceptable reason I heard so far is that these letters will be used with the coming of Mashiach.

Also, these 5 END letters are used only if it falls at the end of the word. If That is true, in the numbering system of the current year 5783=(2022/2023). At this point we are celebrating the year "5783=תשפ"ג:" Once we reach year 5800, it would be then possible to use the letter " 800 = = ף".*Perhaps, putting these 2 logics together, we can expect the coming of Mashiach for another 17 years from the writing of this book?* It would be my honor, if you could share your thoughts, comments or any other information about this or other subjects in this book.

And now for the 28th letter. Here is another amazing fact about the letter *Alef,* in addition to its value of 1, it is also pronounced *Elef* equals 1000. One more fact, as the cherry on top of the cake, it can also be pronounced *Aluf,* which means General, Master, or Champion, which is reserved for *The one & the only*. The circular usage of the letter Alef א .

The BASIC Human
The Fundamental Composition of Humanity

Humanity is a harmonious composition of the tangible and the divine, where the physical body serves as the vessel for the sacred and ethereal soul. This intricate interplay between the material and the spiritual forms the essence of a human being.

Let us embark on a journey through the human body, a marvel of creation, which serves as a conduit for the infusion of the pure and holy soul. This convergence of the physical and the spiritual is a remarkable creation that weaves together the fabric of human existence.

In the wisdom of the Sacred Torah and Sages, we find a profound insight: the human body consists of 248 robust and substantial organs, embodying the resilience of bones and ribs, while harmoniously complemented by 365 delicate and intricate soft tissue organs, encompassing the skin, the heart, and more. The sum of these parts, 248 plus 365, intriguingly amounts to 613, a significant number that resonates with profound meaning. Keep these numerical values in mind, for they are emblematic of a deeper connection.

Delving into the spiritual realm, we encounter an astonishing parallel.

The Torah, a guide to righteous living, presents 248 positive commandments, each mirroring the vitality of our physical organs. Accompanying these are 365 commandments that guide us in abstention, echoing the gentleness of our tender tissues. Astonishingly, each of our 613 body parts finds its counterpart in an associated commandment. The sacred soul and the tangible body unite in an intricate dance, a choreography of existence.

Yet, the soul is the quintessential element that bestows sanctity upon the human experience. It is the point of convergence where the subconscious and the spiritual intersect. This ethereal connection of "Mench", a person of character and virtue, serves to elevate not only oneself but also the world. The purpose of this equilibrium is to enhance the quality of life, to radiate goodness onto oneself and into the lives of others.

In moments of fragility, when a fellow human is ailing, a profound Jewish tradition unfolds. Others gather to offer prayers, beseeching the Divine for complete healing. In these fervent supplications, a heartfelt plea and prayers are offered for the restoration of each of the 613 body parts of the ailing person. This sacred act underscores the symbiotic relationship between the physical and the spiritual. As we petition for well-being, we find renewed inspiration to uphold and embrace the 613 mitzvot, each a thread that weaves us into the tapestry of our physical existence.

This further explains "Am Echad" as all Jews are connected as **ONE** being. The souls of every Jew was present at the moment of receiving the 10 commandments at Mount Sinai. The Soul is considered an eternal and it embodies another object or person, once it departs from its current conduit.

In the symphony of life, each note plays its part, the bodily, the spiritual, the tangible, and the intangible, all meld together to form the beautiful melody of the human experience. As we journey through the intricacies of our existence, may we cherish the unity of body and soul, striving to harmonize our actions with the 613= תרי"ג mitzvot that guide us towards becoming better individuals, enriching our lives while illuminating the world around us.

The HOLINESS act of BABY FORMATION – The Baby Partners

There are three essential partners, who link up together to assemble this wonderful CREATION called **BABY,** eventually MAN.

40 days prior to baby's formation, a Heavenly Voice announces the spouse partner of a baby that still has not even been formed yet! That

means the spiritual bondage is formed long prior to physical formation of the baby.

Below are the 3 partners and what each one brings to table for this miracle formation (in reverse order):

a. **3rd**: **Father,** Provides the seed, semen (color: **White**), which proceeds to transform to all white/light color organs in body, ie. Brain, Bones, Ligaments, the white cells in blood, Nails, Sclera (the white portion of the eye).

b. **2nd: Mother,** Provides the transformation of ALL the **Red** color organs of the baby, such as the meat, red blood cells, muscles, hair, and the dark portion of the eye.

c. **1st:** and foremost **G-Almighty,** who provides for the Soul, Spirit, Wisdom, Intelligence, & all Non-tangible attributes, such as all senses (Hearing, Vision, Smell, Taste, & Touch), Intelligence,...

The father & mother lay down the physical & chemical materials, G-Almighty provides the everlasting, eternal Soul & Spirit to this complex puzzle to a whole one as BABY.

The BELIEF & the CONFIDENCE to G-Almighty is further passed on to the baby while he is enjoying the warmth of mother's womb, by mother's reciting the Torah, Psalms, prayers during the pregnancy. Or by expanding her own horizons as well as that of the BABY at the same time by educating oneself to Jewish learning by searching and listening to thousands of weekly commentaries on Torah.

The mother's Prayers (specially cherished & accepted by G-Almighty) to request from Almighty, that baby is kept in good health during the pregnancy & of course afterward.

What is Judaism? Who is considered a Jew?
Judaism: A Timeless Path of Faith and Belief

Judaism stands as the world's oldest monotheistic religion, its origins dating back over 4000 years. At its core lies an unwavering belief in the oneness of G-Almighty, a belief deeply ingrained in the essence of every Jew, imprinted even before one's physical existence. The memory of forefathers and prophets, revered across the ages, perpetuates this faith.

Central to Judaism is the conviction to the covenant that the One and Only G-Almighty, the Creator of the entire universe, extends His omnipresent love to all. His divine justice rewards virtuous deeds and responds with retribution to transgressions. Throughout history, two magnificent temples were erected and subsequently destroyed, once harboring His Holiness. While the modern era does not afford us the privilege of living amidst these temples and partaking in animal sacrifices, synagogues have emerged as mini-temples, havens where G-Almighty's presence is palpable, requiring devout reverence.

Presently, the global Jewish population numbers around 14 million, with approximately half of them residing in Israel, the heartland of Judaism's contemporary renaissance.

Who is a Jew?

Unveiling the definition of a Jew is pivotal to comprehending the tapestry of Judaism—a faith interwoven with laws, culture, and tradition. To this end, one may be considered Jewish under the following circumstances:

1. **Maternal Descent:** A child born to a Jewish mother inherits Jewish lineage.

2. **Conversion:** An individual, on his/her own will and initiation, may choose to embrace Judaism by adopting its laws, rituals, and practices, thereby accepting the mantle of responsibility for the 613 mitzvot. The conversion process is one of the most stringent processes including a seriously difficult final exam. The person delves into learning the codes

of Torah, while exams and evaluates the new way of living, traditions and culture to match his/her own new identity. After rigorous learning, the convert will have to pass a harsh final exam that a Natural Born Jew, would most probably fail!

Judaism, A Faith Forged in Pillars of Belief & Confidence
Delving further, it is imperative to recognize the foundational pillars that are inherent to every Jewish soul, woven into the fabric of existence from the earliest stages of life, prior to even accepting the known physical form:

1. **Belief in G-A:** The bedrock of Judaism rests upon an unwavering belief in G-Almighty, an entity beyond comprehension yet inherently understood. The belief that our minds and understandings are so limited by time & place, that we can not realize G-Almighty's plans & actions.
2. **Confidence in G-A:** This pillar is the embodiment of trust

in G-Almighty's benevolent guidance, a steadfastly assurance that his Omnipresence is GOOD and he only wants good for all his creations regardless of any subject you might think of. It is the sound mind that one believes that Almighty is his spiritual father, who cares every moment of one's life. Since our conceptual understanding is so limited due to the fact that we are utilizing our brain at a minimum capacity.

Judaism beckons as a timeless path, inviting the curious, the seekers, and the faithful to traverse its rich landscapes. From the echoes of ancient history to the vitality of contemporary practice, Judaism's significance remains undiminished. As we explore its myriad aspects throughout this book, may you find illumination, inspiration, and an enhanced understanding of the intricate tapestry that is the Jewish faith.

The important Role of Women in Judaism

The role of women in Judaism is multifaceted and has evolved over time, influenced by religious texts, cultural contexts, and interpretations. Judaism places a strong emphasis on the equality and inherent value of all individuals, regardless of gender, as they are all created in the image of God. However, traditional interpretations of Jewish law (Halakha) have often assigned distinct roles and responsibilities to men and women within the community.

It is understood that the Torah was given to Israelites in the merit of the women. While in Egypt, the men were being used as slaves, following extremely hard work conditions. When the men would come back home after 16-20 hours work days, they would be so tired (the Masters wishes) that they would not be interested in anything but sleeping. The women would prepare themselves so they would be attractive to their husbands to perform one of the first commandments, Genesis 1:28- "You shall be Fruitful & Multiply". For the merit of this important role they performed in bondage, G-Almighty gave the Torah to Humanity.

Historically, women's roles in Judaism have been centered around home and family life. They have been responsible for maintaining the household, raising children, and observing religious rituals associated with the home, such as lighting the Sabbath candles, preparing kosher meals, and maintaining a kosher home.

In the synagogue, which traditionally has been a male-focused space, women's participation is highly encouraged. Although men traditionally lead the prayer services and Torah readings.

However, in modern times, there has been a significant shift towards greater inclusion and participation of women in various aspects of Jewish religious life. Many Jewish communities are reevaluating traditional gender roles and seeking ways to integrate women's voices and perspectives more fully.

Orthodox Judaism, which tends to hold more conservative views on gender roles, has also seen some changes. While Orthodox communities generally maintain traditional gender roles in prayer services, some women have sought to create spaces for their own Women prayer groups and Torah study sessions. Women have become a lot more vocal about the Torah's teaching and values. Some Orthodox women have also pursued advanced Torah study and Jewish scholarship, and there is an ongoing discussion about how to integrate their insights into Orthodox practice.

Overall, the role of women in Judaism is complex and dynamic, reflecting a combination of tradition, interpretation, and contemporary values. Different Jewish communities and denominations vary in their approaches to gender roles, and these roles continue to evolve in response to changing societal norms and the desire for greater inclusivity.

Binah = The Intelligence
The Highest Level of Attribute Bestowed Upon Women

The intelligence & wisdom to predict the future is called BINAH בינה. This is a trait that is much more predominant in women than men. As the Woman (Eve) was the last and highest class of subject created in the ladder of creation timeline after MAN of course after bringing to being the Sun, moon, stars, animals in the sky, land and the water.

G-Almighty saw that it is not good for the man to be alone, so he took one of the ribs of the MAN called Adam and created the WOMAN, called Eve. *As such the highest grade of Spiritual trait and attribute, Intelligence & Wisdom was awarded to the last creation, Woman.*

The first example of usage of such a trait is described to us by Sarah asking Avraham to distance Ishmael, the son born to Hagar, Sarah's maid. Ishmael at age 13 was misbehaving to Isaac and this bothered Sarah so much that brought her to beseech Avraham to distance Ishamel asap. Avraham was so distressed and could not decide on this request from his lovely wife. He conferred the issue with G-A, the directive was that Avraham *SHOULD*listen to Sarah and to send away Hagar & Ishmael. Sarah's superior vision of the future, with the extra BINAH, was a lot clearer and crisper than Avraham's.

The next example of such extra intelligence & wisdom to see the future was Rivkah with her husband Isaac wishing to bless his son Esav. She saw the first Isaac's blessing not befitting Esav and she made every effort that Jacob would receive the first blessing.

The remarkable gift of foreseeing the future, known as BINAH בינה in Hebrew, holds a place of profound significance. This trait is more notably pronounced in women than in men. In the grand chronology of creation, the WOMAN was the pinnacle, the final masterpiece, preceded only by the formation of the celestial bodies, the animals, and The MAN.

These instances underscore the significance of BINAH, a celestial endowment more potent in women, as they exercise their unique capacity to perceive beyond the present into the future.

The Holy Land; What is HOLY Anyways?

Through the unfolding of Jewish traditions and life philosophy, a profound backbone of meaning emerges, casting an illuminating light on the essence of the Holy Land, and what it truly means for a place to be deemed "Holy."

The concept of holiness, or "kedusha" in Hebrew, transcends mere physicality. It is a spiritual state of being, an intangible resonance that infuses every facet of existence with significance and purpose. In the context of the Holy Land, this transcendent quality is visible, echoing through its landscapes, its history, and the collective consciousness of its people.

At the heart of Jewish tradition lies the belief that the Divine Presence, the very essence of G-d, is intricately interwoven with the fabric of creation. This belief breathes life into every stone, every tree, and every moment that graces the Holy Land. The land becomes a conduit, a bridge between the earthly realm and the realm of the Divine, a place where the ethereal and the tangible converge.

Jewish life philosophy further amplifies this notion of holiness. The teachings of Judaism emphasize the sanctity of time, the preciousness of human relationships, and the significance of actions that elevate the spirit. Observing the "Shabbat," is a prime example of this philosophy. As the sun sets on Friday evening, a sacred aura envelops the land that can only be felt here in the Holy Land. As families gather to welcome the Sabbath Queen, inviting tranquility and spiritual rejuvenation into their homes.

Through intricate rituals, prayers, and acts of loving-kindness, individuals engage in a dance of sanctification, infusing one's lives with purpose and holiness. The daily rhythm of prayer, the pursuit of justice, and the imperative to care for the vulnerable reflect an unwavering commitment to embodying the Divine attributes and nurturing the holiness within themselves and the world around them.

In this context, the Holy Land becomes a microcosm of this philosophy—a landscape where holiness isn't confined to grand edifices but permeates the air, the soil, and the hearts of its inhabitants. From the Western Wall, a remnant of the ancient Temple in Jerusalem, to the vibrant markets of Tel Aviv, each corner of the Holy Land resonates with the echoes of a people dedicated to cultivating holiness in every moment.

As one traverses the landscapes of Israel, guided by the wisdom of Jewish tradition and spirituality, one uncovers a deeper truth about the nature of holiness. He/ She will come to an understanding that the Holy Land isn't merely a geographical location; it's a spiritual realm where the ordinary is transformed into the extraordinary, and where the mundane becomes infused with the sacred.

In exploring the Jewish traditions and life philosophy, one uncovers the complex bondage of the physical and spiritual together. This journey illuminates one's eyes to witness the extraordinary beauty that emerges when human existence is interwoven with the Divine. Through this lens, the Holy Land takes on a new dimension, a realm where holiness is not just a concept, but a living, breathing reality that beckons us to transcend the ordinary and embrace the extraordinary in every facet of our lives.

Holy Items in Judaism: Symbols of Faith and Tradition
Judaism, one of the world's oldest monotheistic religions, is rich in symbols, rituals, and holy items that have been used for millennia to express faith, identity, and devotion. These items, deeply rooted in tradition and scripture, serve as tangible connections to the Divine, historical events, and the core tenets of Jewish belief. Here's a brief overview of some of the most significant holy items in Judaism:

1. ***Torah Scroll:*** At the heart of Jewish worship is the Torah, the first five books of the Hebrew Bible. Handwritten by skilled

scribes on parchment, the Torah scroll is treated with the utmost reverence. It is stored in the Ark (Aron Kodesh) in synagogues and is read during services using a yad, or pointer, to ensure the parchment remains untouched and unspoiled.

2. ***Tefillin (Phylacteries)***: Worn during weekday morning prayers, tefillin are two black leather boxes containing verses from the Torah. One is bound to the arm, facing the heart, and the other is placed on the forehead. They symbolize the commandment to bind G-Almighty's words "as a sign upon your hands" and "between your eyes" (Deuteronomy 6:8).

3. ***Tallit (Prayer Shawl)***: This rectangular garment, adorned with fringes called tzitzit at its four corners, is worn during prayer. The tzitzit serves as a reminder of the 613 commandments in the Torah.

4. ***Mezuzah***: Affixed to the doorposts of Jewish homes, the mezuzah is a small case containing a parchment inscribed with specific Torah verses. It serves as a reminder of Almighty's presence and protection for the home &tenants .

5. ***Menorah:*** Originally the seven-branched candelabrum used in the Temple in Jerusalem, the menorah is a symbol of the Jewish faith. The Chanukiah, a variation with nine branches, is used during the festival of Hanukkah to commemorate the miracle of the oil.

6. ***Kiddush Cup***: Used during Shabbat and festivals, the Kiddush cup holds wine or grape juice. A blessing, or Kiddush, is recited over it, sanctifying the day.

7. ***Shofar***: Made from a ram's horn, the shofar is blown on Rosh Hashanah (the Jewish New Year) and at the end of Yom Kippur (the Day of Atonement). Its haunting sound serves as a call to repentance and introspection.

8. ***Kippah (Yarmulke):*** This head covering, worn by Jewish men and, in some reform communities by women, is a sign of

respect, separation and acknowledgment of G-Almighty's presence above and the person. Observant Jewish women wear head covers such as scurf or fancy hats.

9. ***Seder Plate:*** Central to the Passover festival, the Seder plate holds symbolic foods, each representing aspects of the Exodus story, where the Israelites were freed from Egyptian slavery.

10. ***Mikveh***: While not an "item" in the traditional sense, the mikveh, or ritual bath, is a crucial aspect of Jewish ritual life. Immersion in the mikveh is used for various purposes, including conversion, purification, and family purity laws.

The holy items of Judaism are not mere artifacts but profound symbols that encapsulate the essence of Jewish beliefs, history, and traditions. They serve as bridges between the Divine and the mundane, the past and the present, and between individual and his community. Through these items, Jews across generations and geographies have expressed their enduring faith and commitment to a covenant that dates back thousands of years.

Unveiling the Mystique of Israel
A Tourist's Guide to the Secrets of Judaism

Embarking on a journey to Israel is a transformative experience, a pilgrimage to an ancient land that resonates with spiritual significance for countless people across the globe. As you traverse the breathtaking landscapes and immerse yourself in the historical sacred land, you may find yourself yearning for something more, an insight into the mystery and mythical essence that makes this small Special piece of land called Israel, the Promised Land, a melting pot of faith, culture and heart.

Amidst the awe-inspiring sights and the echoes of history, there exists a palpable craving for understanding, a desire to unravel the intricate threads that have woven the rich fabric of Judaism and the nation of Israel. This quest for knowledge, however, can be a complicated journey, fraught with uncertainties and unspoken questions. How does one approach the complexities of this ancient culture? Whom can you turn to for insight? How can you ask the right questions without intruding upon the sanctity of another's beliefs or space?

Look no further, welcome to your gateway to enlightenment. This book is your unique opportunity to navigate the terrain of Judaism, to unearth its hidden gems, and to glean profound insights that illuminate the essence of Israel's enduring legacy.

Crafted with the inquisitive curious traveler in mind, this guide is a beacon of clarity amidst the boundless expanse of knowledge and cultural intricacies. It presents to the reader simple, modern, and concise answers to the questions that intrigue one's curiosity and beckon the person to delve deeper into the heart of Israel through the spiritual and cultural state that a Jew keeps next to him all the time as a twin second nature.

Designed as a compass to accompany you on your exploration of the Holy Land, this book serves as your companion, a source of illumination that deciphers the complex concepts of Judaism and brings to light the day-to-day rhythm of a Jewish life. You will gain an understanding of the spiritual compass that guides a Jew's actions and beliefs, and you will witness firsthand the interplay between tradition and contemporary existence.

But this book is not just about knowledge; it's about connection. It's about forging a bridge between the ancient wisdom that has sustained Israel for millennia and the modern world we all inhabit. As you absorb the insights within these pages, you'll find yourself not merely absorbing information but embarking on a journey of empathy, a journey that will allow you to glimpse the soul of Israel and its Jewish people.

Through the pages of this guide, you'll unlock the doors to a deeper appreciation of Israel's unique role in history, as the bearer of the Torch of Knowledge, assistance, and peace. As you venture forth into the land of Israel, armed with the wisdom you've gained from these pages, you'll engage with the people, the stories, and the sites in a profoundly meaningful way.

So, whether you're planning your first visit to Israel or seeking to deepen your connection with this intimate timeless land, prepare to be enriched, enlightened, and inspired. Let the secrets of Judaism and the essence of Israel unfold before you, like an ancient map guiding you to the heart of a culture that has endured, thrived, and left an indelible mark on humanity.

Places in Israel Most Visitors Fail to Visit

While many visitors to Israel explore its popular tourist destinations, there are several lesser-well-known places that often don't receive as much attention but offer unique experiences and insights into the country's culture, history, and natural beauty. Here are a few places in Israel that are often overlooked but are worth considering for a more diverse and immersive travel experience:

1. **The Cave of the Patriarchs and Matriarchs**, located in

Hebron, is a significant religious and historical site in Israel that often goes unnoticed by many visitors. This ancient complex holds profound spiritual and cultural significance as it is the final resting place of biblical figures such as Abraham, Sarah, Isaac, Rebecca, Jacob, and Leah. (Rachel's final resting place monument is located in Beit Lehem, where she passed away, on the way to Israel, while giving birth to the last of the 12 tribes: Benjamin.)

The Cave of the Patriarchs and Matriarchs is a remarkable blend of architectural styles, reflecting its long history of respect and worship. Originally a sacred site for various religious traditions, it has been a synagogue, a church, and a mosque over the centuries. The building's intricate design and interior are a testament to the layers of history and worship that have shaped it.

Despite its historical importance, the Cave of the Patriarchs and Matriarchs can sometimes be overshadowed by more well-known sites. However, it offers visitors a unique opportunity to explore the intersection of faith and history. The complex's significance goes beyond its religious role, it also embodies the complexities of coexistence in the region, as it is both a place of prayer for Jews and Muslims. In a land marked by deep-seated cultural and religious tensions, this site serves as a reminder of the shared heritage that binds different communities together. For a comprehensive understanding of Israel's rich tapestry of faith and history, the Cave of the Patriarchs and Matriarchs is a must-visit destination.

1. ***The Western Stone in Tunnels of Western Wall***, a significant component of the Western Wall in Jerusalem, is a colossal

gigantic ONE-PIECE stone block that forms a part of the retaining wall of the Second Temple complex. This humongous stone is unburied and displayed as part of ongoing archeological excavation to unearth the history of Judaism to unravel the fascinating Holy Temples glory. One's amazement cannot be hidden with the seeing of this astonishing admiration. *This stone Weighs an estimated unimaginable 570 tons) this mammoth magnitude stone is one of the largest building blocks in antiquity known used in any structure even in the modern world structures.* Its origins trace back to the time of Herod the Great, who orchestrated the expansion and renovation of the Second Temple.

*The Western Stone can only be visited by acquiring the "Western Wall Tunnel Tour". It is HIGHLY recommended to reserve the tour prior to visiting Jerusalem. The Western Wall complex itself is open 24*7.*
Please let your tour guide about the reservation and insist on including visiting this astonishing monument display in the world.

Please note the impressive dimensions of this massive stone:

a. Length: Approximately 13.6 meters (44.6 feet) long.
b. Height: It stands about 3.5 meters (11.5 feet) tall.
c. Depth/Width: 3.3 meters (10.8 feet- estimated).

While not one of the classical "Seven Wonders of the World," the Western Stone holds its own marvel. It reflects the incredible engineering accomplishment of its time, showcasing the ability to prepare, transport, and place such massive stones without the modern machinery even available today. The stone's significance lies in its role as a remnant of the sacred and historical site of the Second Temple, drawing countless pilgrims and visitors who marvel at its colossal presence and the rich heritage it represents.

1. ***Machon HaMikdash=The Temple Institute***, is an educational and religious organization located in the Old City of Jerusalem. Founded in 1987, the Institute is dedicated to the study of the First and Second Temples, their history, rituals, and significance, and to the preparation for the building of the Third Temple. Here are some key aspects of the Temple Institute:

a. Educational Role: The Institute serves as a center for research and education about the Temples. It offers educational programs, lectures, and tours, aiming to raise awareness about the central role of the Temple in Jewish life and history.

b. Recreation of Temple Vessels: One of the most notable achievements of the Temple Institute is the recreation of many of the vessels, garments, and instruments used in the Temple service, all made according to the exact specifications detailed in ancient Jewish sources. These include the golden menorah, the table for the showbread, and the Cohen Hagadol's (high priest) garments.

c. Blueprints for the Third Temple: The Institute has developed miniature detailed architectural plans for the construction of the Third Temple, based on biblical, Talmudic, and other traditional Jewish sources. These plans are both symbolic, representing the hope for the eventual rebuilding, and practical, intended to be used if the decision to rebuild is made.

d. Controversy: The Temple Institute's mission is not without controversy. The Temple Mount, where the First and Second Temples once stood, is currently home to the Al-Aqsa Mosque and the Dome of the Rock, two of Islam's holiest sites. Any talk of building a Third Temple is seen by many as a threat to the current status quo and can be a source of tension between Jews and Muslims. The Temple Institute, however, emphasizes its peaceful intentions and the spiritual significance of its work.

e. Library and Publications: The Institute boasts a comprehensive library filled with texts about the Temples. They also publish books and articles on related subjects, furthering the academic and religious study of the Temple.

f. Interactive Museum: The Temple Institute has a museum in Jerusalem where visitors can view the recreated Temple vessels and learn about the history and significance of the Temple through interactive displays.

If the Holy Temples are of your interest, this place is MUST 4U.

1. **Akko (Acre):** Located on the northern coast of Israel, Akko is a historic city with well-preserved remnants of Crusader, Ottoman, and British eras. Its old city, a UNESCO World Heritage Site, features a stunning Crusader fortress, a bustling market, and a fascinating underground city with intricate passageways and chambers.

1. **Ein Gedi:** This oasis is situated along the Dead Sea's eastern shore and offers a lush contrast to the surrounding desert landscape. It's a nature lover's paradise with waterfalls, lush vegetation, and hiking trails, including one that leads to a refreshing dip in natural pools.

1. **Rosh Hanikra:** Located on the Mediterranean coast near the border with Lebanon, Rosh Hanikra features stunning white cliffs and sea caves carved by the relentless waves. A cable

car ride takes you down to explore the grottoes and enjoy breathtaking sea views.

1. **Zikhron Ya'akov:** A charming town in the Carmel Mountains known for its picturesque streets, historic buildings, and wine culture. It's home to one of the oldest wineries in Israel and offers a glimpse into the country's early settlement history.

1. **Beit She'an:** An ancient Roman city with well-preserved ruins showcasing a theater, bathhouses, and a cardo (main street). It's an important archaeological site that gives insight into daily life during the Roman period.

1. **Mitzpe Ramon:** This small town is situated on the edge of the Ramon Crater, a massive geological formation in the Negev Desert. The crater offers breathtaking views, hiking trails, and a chance to experience the desert's unique beauty.

1. **Tzfat (Safed):** Known for its significance in Jewish mysticism (Kabbalah), Tzfat is a hilltop town in northern Israel with a bohemian atmosphere, narrow winding streets, and numerous art galleries.

1. **Bet Guvrin-Maresha National Park:** Located in the Judean Lowlands, this park is a World Heritage Site with an extensive complex of man-made caves used for various purposes throughout history, including ancient dwellings and burial sites.

1. **Timna Park:** Situated in the southern Negev Desert, Timna Park is known for its unique rock formations, including Solomon's Pillars, and its history of copper mining. Visitors can explore the geological wonders and learn about ancient

mining techniques.

1. **Sepphoris (Tzippori):** An archaeological site showcasing the remains of a Roman and Byzantine city with well-preserved mosaics, including a famous mosaic known as the "Mona Lisa of the Galilee."

These are just a few examples of the lesser-known places in Israel that offer enriching and distinctive experiences. Exploring these off-the-beaten-path destinations can provide a deeper understanding of Israel's diverse history, culture, and natural beauty. ***In order to have a bright future, we are forbidden to forget our past.***

Chapter 3

Honoring The Divine Wisdom & Judgement in Sacred Texts
The Ten Commandments
The Basic Ethics of All Nations

The Ten Commandments, also known as the Decalogue, stand as a timeless testament to the fundamental ethics that transcend borders, cultures, and faiths. These ten divine principles, located in the Torah, specifically in the Book of Exodus (Exodus 20:2-17) and the Book of Deuteronomy (Deuteronomy 5:6-21), provide a universal moral framework that has guided humanity's sense of right and wrong for millennia.

Enshrined within the Torah, the sacred text of Judaism, the Ten Commandments are not just a religious code for the Jewish people but a set of ethical guidelines that have found resonance in societies across the globe. Their significance extends far beyond religious doctrine, as they encapsulate principles that form the bedrock of ethical behavior, transcending religious boundaries.

The Israelites received the 10 commandments on Mount Sinai and they were called and considered as the "Chosen Nation" with the responsibility of being the light to the Nations of the World. This grand task mandates Jews to exemplify the principles of justice, compassion and ethical behavior of the ten commandments. This Valore liability is not confined to any one era but endures as a timeless obligation. It underscores the enduring relevance of the ethical and moral teachings embedded in the Ten Commandments, which continues to guide and inspire individuals and nations alike as we journey through the complexities of our interconnected world.

The Ten Commandments address both our relationship with the Divine and our interactions with fellow humans. The first set of commandments emphasizes monotheism, urging the worship of one God and the rejection of idols. This monotheistic belief has profound implications for personal morality and the recognition of the sanctity of life.

The second set of commandments addresses our ethical duties towards others. They prohibit actions such as murder, theft, false testimony, and covetousness. These principles, firmly anchored in respect for human life, truth, and property, have become the cornerstones of legal and moral systems worldwide.

Throughout history, these commandments have been revered, quoted, and adapted in various cultures and belief systems. They have served as the ethical foundation for legal codes, shaping the laws and norms of countless nations. For example, several modern Western nations have adopted the Judaism legal systems values, such as the prohibition against murder and theft into their legal frameworks, reflecting the universal recognition of these principles.

The 10 commandments

The Ten Commandments serve as a bridge between religious and secular ethics. They underscore the importance of values such as honesty, compassion, and respect for others, values that resonate with people of diverse backgrounds and beliefs. As such, they are a testament to the shared moral compass that unites humanity.

In a world characterized by diversity and complexity, the Ten Commandments remain a moral anchor, guiding individuals and societies toward ethical conduct. They remind us that, regardless of our cultural or religious affiliations, certain ethical principles are eternally relevant and universally applicable. As we reflect on these timeless guidelines, let us recognize the profound wisdom they contain and the potential they hold to foster a world rooted in compassion, justice, and ethical conduct, a world that transcends the boundaries of faith and nationality.

The Ten Commandments are a set of ethical and moral principles that play a significant role in Judeo-Christian religious traditions, particularly in Judaism and Christianity. These commandments are traditionally divided into two lists, with the first four focusing on one's relationship with God and the remaining six addressing interpersonal relationships. Here are the Ten Commandments:

First Set of Four Commandments (Relating to God):

1. You shall have no other gods before me.
2. You shall not make for yourself an idol or worship any graven image.
3. You shall not take the name of the Lord your God in vain.
4. Remember the Sabbath day, to keep it holy.
5. You shall not covet anything that belongs to your neighbor.

Second Set of Six Commandments (Relating to Human Relationships): 5. Honor your father and mother.

1. You shall not murder.

1. You shall not commit adultery.

1. You shall not steal.

1. You shall not bear false witness against your neighbor (i.e., you shall not lie about others).

1. You shall not covet anything that belongs to your neighbor.

These commandments are foundational in both the Jewish and Christian faiths and serve as guidelines for ethical behavior and moral conduct. Different religious traditions and denominations may slightly vary in how they number or interpret these commandments, but the core principles remain consistent.

The Torah and Israel: A Nation of Knowledge

In the essence of Jewish culture, you will find the threads of Torah and Israel are intricately woven. The term Torah, often translated as "teaching," holds within it the vast ocean of wisdom that guides and illuminates the path of the Jewish people. Simultaneously, Israel stands as a beacon of light, aptly referred to as "The BOOK Nation," with its profound dedication to knowledge and its preservation.

Throughout the landscape of Jewish education, one finds impressive libraries brimming with a rich collection of holy texts. These institutions, adorned with countless volumes, serve as repositories of timeless knowledge. Here, students and scholars immerse themselves in the teachings of the Torah, plumbing its depths to uncover the wisdom that has guided generations.

In the intimate spaces of a Jewish household, a similar commitment to learning unfurls. Here, the shelves are laden with an array of religious and educational books, their pages resonating with profound insights. These texts not only instruct on the intricacies of Jewish life but also illuminate the path of ethical behavior and compassionate interaction with others. They are blueprints for living a life enriched by the principles of Judaism.

613 Commandments: Nourishing the Soul

Central to the Jewish way of life are the 613 commandments, which form the bedrock of individual and collective conduct. These commandments are not mere rules but intricate pathways that lead to spiritual growth and fulfillment. Divided into 248 positive commandments and 365 negative ones, they encompass the spectrum of human behavior, guiding actions to be taken and those to be refrained from.

The Echo of Every Organ: A Soul-Nourishing Symphony

As a symphony of 613 notes creates a harmonious melody, each commandment resonates with a specific facet of the soul. Just as the human body is composed of 613 organs, the commandments nourish and nurture each aspect of the soul's expression. Through the physical observance of 248 positive commandments & 365 abstention commandments, the soul finds its resonance, and the individual aligns with the divine purpose inherent in each commandment.

Guiding Humanity: A Framework for Ethical Interaction

The tapestry of commandments extends beyond the individual, encompassing a framework for ethical and moral interaction with others. Rooted in compassion, justice, and kindness, these commandments foster a sense of responsibility toward fellow humans, the environment, and all living beings. They cultivate a society founded on the principles of righteousness and empathy.

Universal Wisdom; Torah's Teachings

Jewish teachings extend their embrace to all of humanity through ten Commandments. These universal principles serve as a moral compass for people of every background, transcending religious divides. They beckon individuals to uphold ideals of justice, integrity, and compassion, forging a common bond among humanity.

In the grand symphony of Jewish tradition, the Torah's teachings and Israel's essence converge to form a harmonious melody. This harmony extends from the sacred libraries of educational institutions to the humble bookshelves of Jewish homes, guiding individuals in their journey toward self-discovery, compassion, and a life enriched by divine wisdom.

Education for Generations

The Jewish education & teaching is an important factor **not so well known** in the western world. From kindergarten to higher Jewish education levels of Kollel, Yeshivas, Ulpanot (ladies) & of course universities they culminate in the Jewish religion intertwined in every Jew.

Jewish education is not the normal western education that you think of. Torah is not just a textbook. One of the root meanings of Torah is "Teaching/Education". "Education for Generations".

We are thought & reminded about our rich history, our long journeys through time, itineraries, exact dates, exact events, our physical and mental sufferings, our redemption from Egypt, constantly. From our daily prayers, three times a day, festive holidays, prayers and traditions, our Fasting days remember the destruction of the Holy temples.

The Jewish Holidays are filled with commandments and traditions to REMIND & TEACH our young & the next generation about the Jewish RICH history. Remembering, experiencing the events on the exact date that happened going back to three thousand years ago as if it was just last year!

The Jewish teaching is to "Choose a RAV/Rabbi teacher for yourself", so that you must learn with him & can refer to him for any questions for guidance on how to treat

as a Jew in situations that answers are not so accessible or clear.

The intelligent & integrated teaching process, where the Jewish religion & culture are taught by continuous learning the Torah, the 10 Commandments, Talmud, Gemara, Mishna, ...

To secure a promising future, it's imperative that we remember our past.

The Jewel of Torah: Multifaceted Wisdom Journeying Through the Facets of Torah: A Humble Exploration

Among the cherished beliefs embraced by Judaism is the notion that the Torah encompasses an astonishing 70 facets. Each facet, a unique prism through which divine wisdom shines, unfolds at its own pace and depth, tailored to every individual's unique journey of comprehension and growth. Anchored in tradition and governed by sacred rules, we navigate the labyrinthine passages of Torah, continually striving to grasp its profound teachings.

Yet, as we delve into the depths of Torah, we are reminded of a guiding principle: humility. It is imperative that we resist the temptation to exalt ourselves based on our level of understanding or observance. With every stride forward, we tread the delicate balance of modesty, recognizing that our journey, sailing through the Ocean of Knowledge. Each soul, each heart, has a distinct path and a unique connection with the divine G-Almighty.

In the tapestry of life, threads of human interaction form an intricate pattern. A profound lesson which echoes through time: our interactions must be threaded with sensitivity. We wield the scales of judgment, measuring our modesty in diverse situations. As we engage with fellow travelers on this earthly voyage, we cultivate empathy and respect, nurturing bonds that mirror the divine compassion that envelops us all.

Among the most exquisite and, at times, demanding values nurtured by Jewish tradition is the commitment to embrace positivity unwaveringly.

In every circumstance, we are encouraged to peer through the lens of kindness, generosity, grace and compassion. Let's say, we are driving on the highway, when a fellow driver inadvertently crosses our path, even endangering our life. A Jew must consider a myriad of positive possibilities to give the driver the right of way. Could the hurried stranger who cut ahead in line be racing to an urgent family moment? Perhaps he was hurrying up to take his pregnant wife to hospital to bring a new human being to the world.

As we tread the tapestry of existence, a reflective question arises: who are we, and what are we without the guidance and blessings bestowed by G-Almighty? Imagine if the divine spark of thought, action, and reaction were withheld; could we ascend the peaks we now stand upon? Referencing the enlightening segment, "Who is Human," invites deeper contemplation into our true essence.

From the tender moment of awakening till the tranquil embrace of sleep, a Jewish soul journeys with an unwavering companion: G-A. Amidst life's symphony of moments, G-Almighty's presence is a constant, a timeless partner whispering through the chords of existence. In the whispers of the wind, the symphony of life, and the dance of dreams, this companionship is unbroken, a bond of eternity.

Through the Facets of Torah: Guided by Humility, Illuminated by Positivity, and Nurtured by Divine Connection

As we traverse the myriad facets of Torah, humility remains as the Jewish North Star. The guiding principles of modesty, sensitivity, and positive perspective illuminate our path, infusing our journey with empathy and compassion. G-A's benevolent presence, a constant source of comfort and guidance, intertwines with our essence, enveloping us in an eternal embrace. In this interplay of humility, positivity, and divine connection, we embark upon a soulful voyage, unraveling the boundless wisdom that the facets of Torah hold.

"For a future filled with promise, we must cherish and learn from our past history"

Chapter 4

Jewish Ancestral Heritage Patriarchs & Matriarchs

In the grand fabric of human history, the figures known as the Patriarchs and Matriarchs stand as foundational pillars of the Jewish existence. Their stories, woven across the pages of the Hebrew Bible, serve as a compass guiding the course of Jewish identity, values, and aspirations. This section delves deep into the lives and legacies of these iconic figures, unraveling the threads that connect them to contemporary Jewish existence, spirituality, and intellectual pursuits.

At the heart of this exploration are the Patriarchs; Avraham, Isaac, and Jacob, and the Matriarchs; Sarah, Rivka, Leah, and Rachel. These ancestral luminaries provide not only a genealogical lineage but also a profound spiritual heritage. Their journeys, challenges, and triumphs become touchstones for understanding the dynamics of faith, resilience, and the search for a meaningful relationship with the Divine.

The story of Avraham, the father of monotheism, offers insights into the audacity of belief and the transformative power of taking leaps of faith. His willingness to challenge societal norms and answer the

Divine call to leave his homeland reflects a timeless lesson in the pursuit of a deeper connection with G-Almighty.

The narratives of Isaac and Jacob reveal the intricate interplay of inheritance, sibling relationships, and personal growth. Isaac's binding on the altar and Jacob's wrestling with an angel symbolize some of the moments of existential reckoning, highlighting the struggle for self-discovery and spiritual authenticity that engulfs the Jewish living.

The Matriarchs, equally integral to the narrative, showcase the strength of character, devotion, and the crucial role of women in shaping Jewish destiny. Sarah's resilience in her journey to motherhood, Rivka's wisdom in navigating complex family dynamics, Leah's capacity for transformative love, and Rachel's enduring legacy inspire contemporary discussions on feminism, family, and the essence of womanhood.

As we explore the spiritual and intellectual dimensions of these figures, we discover that their stories resonate far beyond ancient times. The lessons derived from their experiences become a wellspring of insight for modern Jewish individuals seeking to grapple with questions of identity, purpose, and ethical conduct.

In the age of social media and rapid information dissemination, these ancestral narratives serve as a counterbalance to the noise of the present. They invite individuals to engage with profound themes of faith, morality, and the quest for meaning. The legacy of the Patriarchs and Matriarchs challenges contemporary Jews to forge their own paths of spiritual growth while remaining firmly anchored in the heritage passed down through generations.

Through the exploration of the "Patriarchs & Matriarchs," readers will unearth the roots of Jewish identity, discover the enduring relevance of these ancestral figures, and gain insights that enrich their personal journeys. By tracing the footsteps of Avraham's Kindness, Isaac's Bravery, Jacob's Glory, Sarah's Intelligence, Rivka's Wisdom, Leah's Devotion, and Rachel's Legacy, we uncover a timeless well of wisdom that continues to shape the lives and aspirations of Jews around the world.

Patriarchs

It is obvious to learn about the history of any nation, we must refer to the origins & roots going back in the tunnel of time.

Let's take an eye-opening small journey in history of the Jewish people

The pinnacle **ICON** of Jewish life through history are our forefathers, Patriarchs & Matriarchs with each one having unmaterialistic different attribute values that have been embedded in the DNA of each Jew. Our Forefathers are so predominant in the Jewish daily life that they are mentioned at least 3 times in our daily & holiday prayers. While remembering their roles in preparing the backbone of Judaism. Each of our Forefathers have mastered a certain set of G-Almighty specific attributes and have passed it on through the generations to our children & grandchildren. Let's start with:

AVRAHAM, The father of ALL Nations and Humanity.

Avrahamwas the first human being to realize the Almighty's existence & power in running the world. Being the first & the greatest Astronomer, and Physics Master of ALL times by expanding the boundaries of his mind, and time achieved the intelligence and understanding to appreciate that although the Sun, Moon, Stars, & the Planets are amazing elements of nature by themselves, but there is *supernatural* power responsible for all their being & creations.

AVRAHAM is known for the attributes of Kindness, Charity, Goodness, Benevolence and Grace.

Avraham showed and practiced these attributes by setting up tents in the middle of desert, open in all directions so any by-passers and guests will freely enter the tent, relax, drink, eat, with no expectation of receiving any payback for his services. Instead, before the guests would leave the premise, they would thank Avraham for his hospitality, But he would graciously remind them that all he has, as well as ALL the guest enjoyed eating or drinking, belongs to kindness & charity of G-Almighty and the thanksgiving is reserved for him solely and should be offered entirely to G-Almighty & not to himself.

Avraham passed 10 challenging trials during his life with the hardest one "sacrificing his only beloved son, Isaac"

The covenant of CIRCUMCISION & Promise of the Land

Is one of the most observed Jewish commandments performed on all male born. between G-Almighty, Avraham and his generations. Genesis 17:8-16).

(8) "The whole land of Canaan, where you now reside as a foreigner, I will give as an everlasting possession to you and your descendants after you; and I will be their G-Almighty."

(9) Then G-Almighty said to Avraham, "As for you, you must keep my covenant, you and your descendants after you for the generations to come."

(10) "This is my covenant with you and your descendants after you, the covenant you are to keep: Every male among you shall be circumcised."

(11) "You are to undergo circumcision, and it will be the sign of the covenant between me and you."

(12) "For the generations to come every male among you who is eight days old must be circumcised, including those born in your household or bought with money from a foreigner(servants), those who are not your offspring."

(13) "Whether born in your household or bought with your money(servants), they must be circumcised. My covenant in your flesh is to be an everlasting covenant."

(14) "Any uncircumcised male, who has not been circumcised in the flesh, will be cut off from his people; he has broken my covenant."

(15) G-Almighty also said to Avraham, "As for Sarai your wife, you are no longer to call her Sarai; her name will be Sarah."

(16) "I will bless her and will surely give you a son. I will bless her so that she will be the mother of nations; kings of peoples will come from her."

All male infants are circumcised of the extra piece of genital skin (The tip) on the 8th day after he is born. The Mohel (the person who performs the circumcision) makes a number of checks and visits with the baby until the 8th day and afterwards to review the baby's health and progress.

The Mohel often with consultation of the Doctor can make an exception on the 8th day of circumcision to postpone the ceremony until the baby is fit to go through the process.

BTW, I have to emphasize the fact, extra care is given to make sure that the knife used by Mohel is so extra razor sharp, that the baby will feel no pain during the actual circumcision. The pain that the baby feels, usually is alleviated and the incision is healed with the milking process within a couple of days.

Let's not forget the Mohel's role has been with Jews ever since our great, great, grandfather, Avraham, who was the first one to make such a covenant. The process is a very complex task that Mohel goes through a strict learning and practicing process. Some modern parents, due to either trust or preference to a sterile environment, prefer to perform the procedure in Hospital or Doctor's office. Which is absolutely fine. The important thing is to remove the extra skin from the genital organ. Of course, not forgetting the spiritual bondage that this act represents with the proper prayers that should be stated.

The circumcision is considered a very happy occasion (almost for all ☺), celebration followed by a great party that parents arrange.

Part of this jubilee's celebration is due to naming of the Child which is assigned by the parents.The baby's name can be used to call him only after the circumcision.

There is much to be said on the number 8. Why 8th day and not 10? 15, The number 7 is considered a natural number, ie. 7 days a week. The number 8 is considered to be a super natural number. Avraham circumcised Isaac, his son on the 8th day as a supernatural act between humans and the Omnipresence.

Modern science has shown and proven that a baby starting on the 8th day of his birth has the best and largest amount of immune material in his body to protect him from the circumcision process.

Although some people look at the circumcision process as an act of inhumane and causing pain for the baby, spiritually this process is a lot more complex and beyond what our eyes see. The circumcision is a ceremonial bound and covenant commandment with G-Almighty.

Avraham's Servant (Eliezer) finding a wife for his beloved son, Isaac

Avraham sent his servant (known as EliEzer) to his family in Haran to find a wife for his beloved son Isaac, to make sure that he would not marry a Canaanite woman. Eliezer took many expensive gifts to give to the intended bride and went to Aram Naharayim to fulfill his master's wish.

EliEzer requested G-A assistance in this important venture to find a bride for his Master's son. He made a covenant with G-A, should show him the first girl who offers and shows her compassion not only to him, but also to the herd. This covenant was made narrowed down further, that she should also offer him a place to sleep, eat & drink!

The girl who can show so much empathy, kindness and tenderness in understanding the situation even to think of the herd, would be the bride that he has come to search for as Avraham's commandment. As her traits are worthily suited to the attributes of his Master's son.

While he was waiting at the well outside of the city. A beautiful girl, Rivka (known only as 3 years old) offers him not only all the comforts for the guest, but also showing her sympathetic humanistic attribute of understanding even to the camel's need to have traveled such a long way, while providing the badly needed drink & food for all the animals *single handedly*.

The Torah portion reading of this fascinating story is **Chayee Sarah, book of Genesis (24,1)**. The Shabbat that this portion of the Torah is read, usually falls in October or November, attracts Jews (known as 50,000+) from all over the world to Hebron, the city of our forefathers.

The merit and virtue of this Significant Shabbat event is so symbolic in Jewish culture and tradition that all singles approach to this historic place closest possible to our forefathers who can appeal to G-Almighty on their behalf for the proper companion in life. The spiritual presence of the forefathers is such an uplifting event that words cannot explain the emotions. Sorry; The magnitude of spiritual experience can be grasped and achieved through personal encounters ONLY. This is one of those "You have to be there!"

ISAAC
Symbol of "Bravery, Heroism, Courage, Valor, Fortitude, & Strength"

The story of Isaac's, son of Avraham and Sarah sacrifice saga journey at age 37, who joined his father Avraham to the uncharted & undetermined voyage knowing well what destiny has set for him. *"His Own Sacrifice for G-Almighty"*

Avraham's absolute loyalty with the resolute passion of sacrificing his ONLY beloved son, only child of his beloved wife, Sarah, who they both had waited for so long. Avraham was 100 years old when Isaac was born. G-A commanded Avraham to sacrifice his 37 years old son. The successful passing of Avraham's trial was an absolute test of assessment of Avraham's honest loyalty and confidence to G-A.

Once reaching the destination, Avraham restrained his beloved son, Isaac by tying him up to the altar and tree branches around him, in order to commence G-A commandment, whole heartedly, happily!!! All while Isaac (reminder, think of it, 37 years old) showing his special attributes of ***bravery & strength***, by resting on the woods, endorsed himself to his father's wishes, by showing his loyalty & assurance to G-A. He requested his father to fasten his legs strongly to the altar, so when his soul leaves his body, he would not disrespect him by not having control on his legs and G-d forbid, his feet would sin by hitting him!.

His request was two-folded as he would not want to regret at the last minute and turn himself loose and this way show disrespect to his father & his wishes at the critical time of sacrifice. Isaac, known by the attribute of Bravery, was ready to accept any outcome!!! Vow; What a dedication and devotedness to G-A's commandment. ***No FEAR from ANYTHING, just FEAR of G-Almighty alone!!!***

This commandment was (fortunately for all humanity) abruptly canceled by Angels at the last moment to show G-Almighty's acceptance of Avraham's loyalty & confidence from one side & the act of Isaac's bravery and courage on the other side of the spectrum.

I am sure sometime in the near future when scientists can analyze the genes of a man and pinpoint such attributes in our DNA.

The story of Isaac's binding, found in the Book of Genesis in the Bible, is a powerful narrative that explores themes of faith, devotion, and courage. Isaac, the son of Avraham and Sarah, plays a central role in this story as he willingly participates in his father's test of faith.

At the heart of the story is Avraham's unquestioning obedience to G-Almighty's command to sacrifice his beloved son. Despite the emotional turmoil and moral dilemmas this command presents, Avraham displays unwavering loyalty and trust in G-Almighty. This willingness to follow divine instructions, even when they seem contradictory to human values, serves as a testament to Avraham's faith.

Isaac, too, demonstrates remarkable qualities in this narrative. His willingness to comply with his father's actions and trust in God's plan showcase his own dedication to fulfilling divine will. Isaac's act of submitting to his father's intentions and submitting to being bound on the altar reveal his inner strength and courage. His request to be tied securely to avoid any change of heart exemplifies his unwavering resolve.

The narrative reaches a critical moment when an angel intervenes, preventing the sacrifice and affirming Avraham's commitment and Isaac's readiness. This intervention underscores the significance of faith and devotion of humans.

Throughout history, the story of Isaac's binding has been interpreted in various ways. It has been seen as a test of Avraham's loyalty, a lesson in obedience, and a demonstration of both fatherly love and divine compassion. It continues to resonate with individuals as a source of moral and spiritual reflection, inspiring discussions about the nature of faith and sacrifice.

As you alluded, the story of Isaac's binding could serve as a symbol of certain attributes, such as bravery, courage, and devotion, that individuals may admire and aspire to. While genetics may contribute to certain personality traits, it's important to recognize the broader context in which such attributes are developed and nurtured. The story invites us to consider the complex interplay of individual choice, upbringing, values, and faith in shaping our character.

Isaac's blessing saga of Jacob & Esau

Isaac, at his old age, barely having the ability to see, wants to bless his first-born son; his request to Esav was to prepare for him food so that he can bless him. Esav who had already sold his first-born rights to his younger brother, Jacob as depicted in Bible, book of Genesis 25:29-34 (saga by itself). Rivka/Rebecca, Isaac's wife, was put into a unique decision making that would affect ALL generations in the future.

Rivka knows well that Esav was a deceiving person who possessed unfit Jewish attributes. She assists Jacob to receive Isaac's blessing prior to Esav coming back from the hunting venture.

After Jacob receives his father's blessing with the prepared food by his mother, Esav shows up with animals he hunted and it becomes clear to him that he has been deceived from receiving his father's first blessings. At which point, Esav decides that he is the staunch enemy of Jacob, whom he has simply to kill.

The saga of Isaac's blessing of his sons, Jacob and Esav, is a significant and complex story found in the Book of Genesis in the Bible. This narrative, often referred to as the "Blessing of Jacob," explores themes of family dynamics, deception, divine providence, and the consequences of choices made.

At the heart of the story is Isaac, who is nearing the end of his life and wishes to bless his eldest son, Esav. However, Esav had previously sold his first birthright to his younger twin brother, Jacob, in exchange for a bowl of lentil stew. This transaction signaled a transfer of the spiritual privileges and responsibilities of the firstborn to Jacob.

Rivka (Rebecca), Isaac's wife, plays a central role in the narrative. She is aware of Esav's negative character and Jacob's positive qualities, and she takes decisive action to ensure that Jacob receives the blessing intended for the firstborn. She instructs Jacob to disguise himself as Esav and bring her a meal, which she then prepares and presents to Isaac. Since Esav was a heavily hairy person, she takes the skin of sheep and puts it on Jacob's arms as if he is Esav.

Since Isaac's eyesight was extremely minimal, uncertain about the identity of the person standing before him, he touches the arms of Jacob, thinking that he is touching Esav's hands. Isaac initially blesses Jacob, believing him to be Esav. This blessing includes a request for divine favor, abundant resources, and authority over his brother.

When Esav returns and realizes that Jacob has received the blessing, he is filled with anger and resentment. Esav's reaction reflects his impulsive and emotional nature. He vows to kill Jacob, prompting Rivka to intervene again to protect Jacob. She advises Jacob to flee to her family in Haran until Esav's anger subdued, until.a later date when Jacob would be safe from Esav's devious intentions.

The saga of Isaac's blessing serves as a pivotal moment in the biblical narrative, with far-reaching implications for the development of the Israelite nation. It highlights the complexities of family relationships, the moral dilemmas posed by deception, and the role of divine providence in shaping the course of events.

This story also reflects broader themes of inheritance, destiny, and the consequences of choices made by individuals and their descendants. The characters' actions and decisions contribute to the unfolding drama and set the stage for future events in the biblical narrative.

YAACOV/JACOB

Next in line of our ancestor forefathers is *JACOB*, who introduced *the attribute of Majestic Glory and Magnificence to humanity (a combination of Avraham & Isaac merits together)*. Jacob, son of Isaac & Rivka, grandson of Avraham and Sarah.

Jacob was a highly spiritual person even while he was in mother's womb. He would always strive to be as close as practically possible to G-Almighty Magnificent Devine and Might and Spirit.

While Rivka was pregnant with twins, when passing by the holy places, *Jacob* would show so much energy and anxiety that he wanted to jump out to be as close as possible to G-Almighty. While his twin brother *Esav*, would show the same anxiety and restlessness to join and link up to the dark forces and places of idol worship.

Almighty's Art Gallery ©

Jacob's Ladder Dream (Genesis 28:10-19)

In the intricate tapestry of biblical narratives, the account of Jacob's Ladder Dream stands as a pivotal moment in the life of Jacob, a central figure in the lineage of the Israelite patriarchs. This story, nestled within the pages of the Book of Genesis, offers profound insights into the divine-human encounter and the enduring covenant between God and His chosen people.

Jacob, the son of Isaac and the grandson of Abraham, finds himself on a transformative journey to Paddan Aram, the ancestral homeland of his mother, Rebekah. His sojourn is laden with profound significance, for it marks the beginning of a journey both physical and spiritual. Along the way, weary from the day's travels, Jacob selects a simple stone as a pillow and lays down for the night. Little does he know that this seemingly ordinary choice of rest would become the setting for a divine revelation of extraordinary magnitude.

As Jacob slumbers under the starry canopy of the night sky, his mind becomes a conduit for the divine. In his dream, he witnesses an awe-inspiring sight—a ladder, resembling a stairway, spans the chasm between Earth and Heaven. This celestial staircase serves as a conduit for celestial messengers, angels, who ascend and descend upon it. Above the ladder stands the Omnipresence, radiating with divine majesty.

Jacob's dream is not merely a vision of cosmic architecture but a symbolic representation of the connection between the earthly realm and the heavenly sphere. The ladder signifies the bridge between humanity and the divine, and the angels symbolize the intermediaries between God and mortals. This dream reinforces the idea that God is not distant or detached from His creation but is actively engaged in the affairs of humanity, sending messengers to carry out His divine will.

In the midst of this celestial spectacle, God Himself speaks to Jacob, reaffirming the covenant established with his forebears, Abraham and Isaac. The Lord's words are a promise of immeasurable blessings: land as an inheritance, a multitude of descendants, and divine protection. This divine covenant underscores the enduring nature of God's commitment to the chosen lineage and serves as a reminder that the divine plan for the descendants of Abraham continues through Jacob and his descendants.

Upon awakening from his dream, Jacob is profoundly moved by the encounter with the divine. He recognizes the sanctity of the place, which he dubs "Bethel," meaning "the house of God." This naming ceremony is not a mere act of nomenclature but a declaration of the profound spiritual experience Jacob has undergone. It signifies the transformation of an ordinary location into a sacred space—a place where heaven and earth intersect, and the presence of the divine is palpable.

Jacob's Ladder Dream encapsulates the essence of faith, revelation, and the enduring covenant between God and His people. It serves as a reminder that, even in the mundane moments of life, divine encounters can occur, reshaping our understanding of the world and our place within it. Jacob's journey and dream illuminate the path of spiritual growth and the profound truth that God's promises are unwavering and everlasting. This sacred narrative continues to resonate with believers, inspiring them to seek their own "Bethel" moments—encounters with the divine that transform ordinary existence into a profound and sacred journey.

Jacob's Fighting the Angel (Genesis 32:22-32)
ISRAEL=Another Name of JACOB

When Jacob is returning to Canaan with his family and possessions. He learns that his estranged brother, Esav, is coming to meet him with 400 men. Jacob is filled with fear and prays for protection from G-Almighty.

That night, Jacob sends his family across the Jabbok River and remains alone on the other side. During the night, he wrestles with a mysterious spiritual figure, often interpreted as an angel or divine being. They wrestle until daybreak, and Jacob refuses to let go unless the Angel blesses him. In response, the figure blesses Jacob and changes his name to Israel, which means "he who struggles with G-Almighty."

The reason for Jacob's wrestling with the angel is symbolic and multifaceted. It represents Jacob's personal struggle, transformation, and reconciliation. Some interpretations suggest that it also symbolizes Jacob's wrestling with his past, including his deception of his father, Isaac, and his brother, Esav. Jacob's name change to Israel signifies a new identity and a new relationship with G-Almighty. While Jacob is promised to be the father of Am Echad.

His role as the father of the 12 Tribes nation of Israel, has taught us so much on understanding, limiting the desire, being patient & content, while exercising restrain the passion for what one needs or wishes for.

Jacobs First Love - Rachel

Here is Jacob's 14 years love story that can make a legendary full screen movie. Jacob started an escape journey from Esav, by going to Haran where his uncle Lavan HaArami (Rivka's brother) lived. Once Jacob reached the destination, waiting by a well, he saw a number of farmers & peasants who brought all their large herds and flocks to water.

Then he saw the love of his life time, Rachal, whose beauty was second to none. She waited until everyone finished giving water to their animals, then she started to take care of her herd.Jacob requests from Lavan the hands of Rachal to marry, the younger of the two sisters. Lavan agrees with the condition that Jacob will work for him for a period of 7 years before he can marry Rachal.

Lavan was informed that Jacob had received his father's first-born blessing & in turn All the wealth Avraham left for Isaac, passed on to Jacob. Lavan has been described in the bible as a deceptive, deceitful, fraudulent, and unfair person. Jacob worked very hard for Lavan for the period of 7 years. On commencement, Lavan prepared a wedding. Unbeknown to Jacob, the marriage ceremony took place with Leah, older sister, much less attractive than Rachel due to Leah's eye vision problems.

When Jacob asked Lavan the reason for this awkward act, Lavan told him, it is not customary for the younger girl to get married before the older daughter. Lavan was so crooked that he had an instant answer & solution to the problem: "since you have been working so well for me loyally (as you have brought me so much blessing by the fact of your presence); You can continue working for another 7 years for me so you can marry both daughters.

Jacob, compelled & strained by the tremendous passion, fondness, enthusiasm & love of Rachel, succumbs for another 7 years of working for Lavan. Meaning in turn, Jacob worked 14 years to marry Rachel. This marriage was packaged with Rachel, Leah, and their two maidservants, a total of four wives. Jacob & his 4 wives parented the 12 children or 12 Israelites tribes.

Jacob & Yossef (Joseph) Meeting after 22 agonizing years

The last two children of Jacob were born to Rachel; Yossef & Benyamin. ***Yossef, (Master of Dreams)*** so dearly loved by Jacob was envied by his 10 brothers, for his outrageous dreams of envisioning himself as their leader in future.

These dreams were so overwhelming that it lit the fire of hate and detest in brothers up to the point they collectively decided to kill him one day as he approached them in the fields away from their father.

While Yossef was eventually sold to Egyptians merchants as a slave, the brothers deceitfully brought Yossef's cloth torn, laced with the blood of sheep to Jacob. The brothers informed Jacob that his favorite son, "Yossef has been killed by a savage animal."

Jacob's next reunion with Joseph was after 22 years, when Israelites, go to Egypt, Goshen to start a livelihood (running away from famine) by the order of Yossef, who had eventually become the most powerful person in Egypt followed after Paroh.

Jacob's 22 agonizing years of separation from his favorite son, Joseph, teaches us the value of patience and confidence in G-Almighty. He never lost the hope even one minute that one day he will have the joy of seeing Joseph.

The Deed & Promise of Promised Land to Patriarchs & Beyond

The Promise of Promised Land To Patriarchs in Torah.

The concept of the Promised Land for the Israelites is a central theme in the Torah. It refers to the Holy land that God promised to give to the descendants of Avraham, Isaac, and Jacob throughout the pages of Torah etched by G-Almighty. :

Here are the key passages from the Torah that discuss the Promised Holy Land to the Israelites, along with their corresponding text:

1.   God's Promise to Avraham:

Genesis 12:1-3: "The Lord had said to Abram, 'Go from your country, your people and your father's household to the land I will show you. I will make you into a great nation, and I will bless you; I will make your name great, and you will be a blessing. I will bless those who bless you, and whoever curses you I will curse; and all peoples on earth will be blessed through you.'"

1. *Renewal of the Promise to Isaac:*

Genesis 26:1-5: "Now there was a famine in the land—besides the previous famine in Avraham's time—and Isaac went to Avimelech, king of the Philistines in Gerar. The Lord appeared to Isaac and said, 'Do not go down to Egypt; live in the land where I tell you to live. Stay in this land for a while, and I will be with you and will bless you. For you and your descendants I will give all these lands and will confirm the oath I swore to your father Avraham. I will make your descendants as numerous as the stars in the sky and will give them all these lands, and through your offspring all nations on earth will be blessed, because Avraham obeyed me and did everything, I required of him, keeping my commands, my decrees and my instructions.'"

1. *God's Covenant with Jacob:*

Genesis 28:13-15: "There above it stood the Lord, and he said: 'I am the Lord, the God of your father Avraham and the God of Isaac. I will give you and your descendants the land on which you are lying. Your descendants will be like the dust of the earth, and you will spread out to the west and to the east, to the north and to the south. All peoples on earth will be blessed through you and your offspring. I am with you and will watch over you wherever you go, and I will bring you back to this land. I will not leave you until I have done what I have promised you.'"

1. The Land Promised to Avraham, Isaac, and Jacob:

Genesis 35:9-12: "After Jacob returned from Paddan Aram, God appeared to him again and blessed him. God said to him, 'Your name is Jacob, but you will no longer be called Jacob; your name will be Israel.' So, he named him Israel. And God said to him, 'I am God Almighty; be fruitful and increase in number. A nation and a community of nations will come from you, and kings will be among your descendants. The land I gave to Avraham and Isaac I also give to you, and I will give this land to your descendants after you.'"

1. The Exodus and the Promised Land:

Exodus 3:7-10: "The G-Almighty said, 'I have indeed seen the misery of my people in Egypt. I have heard them crying out because of their slave drivers, and I am concerned about their suffering. So, I have come down to rescue them from the hand of the Egyptians and to bring them up out of that land into a good and spacious land, a land flowing with milk and honey—the home of the Canaanites, Hittites, Amorites, Perizzites, and Hivites. And now the cry of the Israelites has reached me, and I have seen the way the Egyptians are oppressing them. So now, go. I am sending you to Pharaoh to bring my people the Israelites out of Egypt.'"

1. The Exodus and the Promised Land (Continued):

Exodus 6:6-8: "Therefore, say to the Israelites: 'I am the Lord, and I will bring you out from under the yoke of the Egyptians. I will free you from being slaves to them, and I will redeem you with an outstretched arm and with mighty acts of judgment. I will take you as my own people, and I will be your God. Then you will know that I am the G-A your G-d, who brought you out from under the yoke of the Egyptians. And I will bring you to the land I swore with an uplifted hand to give to Avraham, to Isaac and to Jacob. I will give it to you as a possession. I am the G-Almighty.'"

1. *The Land as an Inheritance:*

Numbers 34:1-12: "The Lord said to Moses, 'Command the Israelites and say to them: "When you enter Canaan, the land that will be allotted to you as an inheritance is to have the specific boundaries that even now can be traced in today's Geographic locations. "This will be your land, with its boundaries on every side.'"

1. *Moses' Last Words About the Land:*

Deuteronomy 1:7-8: "Break camp and advance into the hill country of the Amorites; go to all the neighboring peoples in the Arabah, in the mountains, in the western foothills, in the Negev and along the coast, to the land of the Canaanites and to Lebanon, as far as the great river, the Euphrates. See, I have given you this land. Go in and take possession of the land the Lord swore he would give to your fathers, to Avraham, Isaac, and Jacob, and to their descendants after them.'"

Deuteronomy 3:18-20: "At that time I commanded you: 'The G-Almighty has given you this land to take possession of it. But all your able-bodied men, armed for battle, must cross over ahead of the other Israelites. However, your wives, your children and your livestock may stay in the towns I have given you, until the Lord gives rest to your fellow Israelites as he has to you, and they too have taken over the land that the G-Almighty your G-d is giving them across the Jordan. After that, each of you may go back to the possession I have given you.'"

These passages highlight the significance of the Promised Land in the Torah and the covenantal relationship between G-Almighty and the descendants of Avraham, Isaac, and Jacob. ***They all collectively convey the idea that the Promised Land, the Holy Land, was an*** *inheritance from God to the descendants of Avraham, Isaac, and Jacob*. The journey of the Israelites toward the Promised Holy Land is a central narrative in the Torah and serves as a foundational story in Jewish tradition

The Promise of Promised Land - Beyond the Torah,

In addition to the Holy scripture Torah evident, the concept of the Holy Promised Land and its significance to the Israelites is mentioned and discussed in various other books of the Hebrew and Jewish literature. Here are a few examples:

1. *Joshua:*

The Book of Joshua chronicles the Israelites' conquest of the Promised Land under the leadership of Joshua after the death of Moses. It describes the division of the land among the tribes of Israel and the fulfillment of God's promise to give them the land.

1. *Psalms:*

The Psalms contain numerous references to the Promised Land, expressing longing, gratitude, and praise for God's gift of the land to the Israelites. Psalm 105, for instance, provides a poetic account of God's covenant with Avraham and the journey to the Promised Land.

1. *Prophetic Books*:

The Prophets frequently reference the Promised Land in their messages, often using it as a metaphor for spiritual renewal and restoration. The books of Isaiah, Jeremiah, Ezekiel, and others convey the idea that the return to the land is symbolic of God's faithfulness and the restoration of the people.

1. *Rabbinic and Midrashic Literature:*

Jewish rabbinic and Midrashic(explanatory) literature, such as the Midrash Rabbah and Talmud, expand on the themes of the Promised Land. They offer interpretations, insights,

and discussions about the significance of the land in the context of Jewish law, ethics, and theology.

1. *Jewish Services and Prayers*:

Jewish prayers and services make many references to the Promised Land. For example, the Amidah (the central prayer in Jewish worship) includes requests for the restoration of Jerusalem and the ingathering of the exiles to the land.

1. *Book of Kings 1 & 2:*

Books of Kings 1 & 2, and Divrei Yamim (Chronicles) recount the historical events of the Israelites' settlement in the land, the construction of the First and Second Temples in Jerusalem, and the periods of exile.

1. *Modern Jewish Thought and Literature:*

Throughout Jewish history, the concept of the Promised Land has continued to be a significant theme in Jewish thought, literature, and cultural expressions. It is often explored in the context of Zionism, the modern movement advocating for a Jewish homeland in Israel.

MATRIARCHS

Sarah is the first biblical matriarch and prophetess, a major figure in Abrahamic Jewish religions. While different Abrahamic faiths portray her differently, Judaism, Christianity, and Islam all depict her character similarly, as that of a most divine, mystic and spiritual pious woman, devoted, renowned for her hospitality, kindness and beauty, glamorously appealing and attractiveness, the wife and half-sister of Avraham.

Sarah's surpassed beauty was so overwhelming irresistible that two different Kings)Pharaoh& Abimelech) wanted to possess her, while she was already devoted to the marriage bound with Avraham. The custom of times was such that they would respect the married woman by not making advances to her. Although if no husband was in the picture, the story would be a bit different. As such, if someone and of course, when the person of such stature importance & prominence as a King in such a situation would advise his bodyguards to practice the "Houdini disappearing act with the husband". And Walla; Problem solved.

In both situations, Avraham requests from Sarah that she would please introduce herself as his sister & not her husband, so that the king will spare his life. BTW, you might say; wait, that means he asked her to lie and if lying is dishonest and forbidden, how can two of the most prominent people in such stature lie? There are at least two points that I would like to bring to your attention. First, no lies spoken by Avraham or Sarah since they were half-brothers & sisters. Second, there are times that white lies are allowed if lives are in danger.

Sarah's new name was elevated from Sarai שרי at the age of 90 Years Young. While Avraham's name was uplifted at age 99 from Avram, אברם . Both their names were uplifted by The Divine G-Almighty to their new names to make the first of the three covenants that G-A with Jewish people.

This name change was performed by the holy one by removing the letter "י" from Sarah's name = 10, splitting it in two equals which is 5 = "ה", while adding the letter "ה" to names of both Avram & Sarai for their new names Avraham & Sarah.

The letter "ה" also ascertains the name of G-Almighty in alphabet, was specifically added to their names to show the level and elevations of their holiness. It is seriously believed that this was the key and the virtue for their blessings to change their barren status to fruitfully bringing Isaac to the world.

Rivka - Rebbeca

Is a biblical figure appearing in Genesis, the second in the four mothers of the people of Israel. The daughter of Bethuel and the sister of Lavan Harami, Isaac's wife, the mother of twins Jacob and Esav. Although her name has been least mentioned from the Matriarchs in the bible, there are a number of important events in which her predominant influential role is evidenced.

Rivka is remembered as a woman of strength, resourcefulness, and pivotal importance in the early history of the Jewish people. Her story highlights themes of divine providence, family dynamics, and the importance of faith in the biblical narrative. She is revered as one of the matriarchs of the Jewish tradition and is often cited as an example of a woman of great faith and purpose in the Bible.

Rachel

Rachel is THE most favorite of the four wives of Jacob. As explained earlier in Jacob's section, once Jacob realized the ill-intentions of his father-in-law Lavan, after 22 years, he gathered all his belongings and his 4 wives upon vision of angels in advising him to get out from Haran and go back to the land of his father, Isaac.

Once Lavan found out that Jacob, with his wives, children, and flocks had run away, he followed Jacob and caught them upon Gilad Mountains. Lavan was very upset and asked him why did you steal my daughters, belongings and worst of all, his Idol G-D.

Jacob told him of his scary thoughts of Lavan's intentions and told him, I never stole anything from you during all these years. " And unbeknown to him of Rachel's act, he swears: **"Whoever who stole your idol should not live within us"**. Please see below *"The Power of Words: A Cautionary Tale"* on this important issue.

Tragically, Rachel's life was cut short during childbirth of her second son, Benjamin in Bethlehem on the way prior to reaching their destination, Israel. Her resting place along the road to Bethlehem is a site of pilgrimage and prayer, a place where generations would come to seek solace and inspiration.

Rachel, a luminous figure in the tapestry of Jewish history, emerges as a symbol of enduring love and unwavering faith. Her story weaves through the pages of the Torah, leaving an indelible and unerasable mark on the hearts of those who seek to learn of her stature and grace.

As the beloved wife of Jacob, Rachel's journey unfolds with both joys and trials. Her initial encounter with Jacob at the well, where she assisted him in watering his flock, sets the stage for a love story that transcends time. Their connection was immediate and profound, a divine union guided by destiny.

Yet, Rachel's path was not without hardship. Despite Jacob's love, she faced the heartache of infertility, a poignant challenge in a culture that placed great importance on bearing children. Her sister Leah's ability to conceive more & more children further intensified her pain.

In a selfless act of compassion, Rachel offered her handmaid Bilhah to Jacob to conceive children for her. This act of sacrifice and love demonstrates her profound devotion to Jacob's lineage, even as she endured personal anguish. In addition to Bilhah, Jacob also married Zilpa, who was Leah's maidservant.

Only after Jacob had 10 children from 3 of his wives, Rachal was awarded with the last two tribes: Joseph and Benjamin.

Rachel's unbreakable bond with Jacob extended to her role as a matriarch, guiding her descendants through the trials and triumphs of generations. Her legacy lives on through her son Joseph, who rises to great prominence in Egypt.

Rachel's enduring spirit, her unyielding love, and her unshakeable faith continue to resonate with people around the world. Her story serves as a beacon of hope, reminding us of the power of love, sacrifice, and unwavering devotion in the face of life's trials.

The legacy of Rachel urges us to treat our words with the reverence they deserve. It prompts us to cultivate the art of speaking thoughtfully, compassionately, and responsibly. In a world that often celebrates the loud and the brash, we are reminded that true strength lies in the ability to harness our words for positive impact.

As we navigate the intricate dance of human interaction, let us strive to honor the values of Judaism by becoming stewards of our speech. Let us choose words that reflect the teachings of empathy, understanding, and connection. And let us remember that, much like the pebble dropped into a pond, our words create ripples that extend far beyond the moment of utterance. In this way, we can harness the power of words to contribute to a world rich in goodness, compassion, and lasting harmony.

Leah

Leah &Rachal daughters of Lavan Arami (Rivka's Brother) is mother of 6 of the Israelites tribes. There is belief that Rachel was Leah's younger twin sister. Further belief, that they were supposed to marry the twins of Esav & Jacob. In a way Esav's hate for Jacob was further flamed by the fact that Jacob married with both twins.

Leah's spiritual levels were of the highest possible. With a terrible thought of having to marry Esav (first born as well), she cried so much that her eye vision was reduced to minimal.

Leah's attributes are known to be her loyalty and devotion to her husband Jacob and her family. As such she was the most fruitful of the 4 Matriarchs with 6 children: Reuven, Shimon, Levi, Yehuda, Issachar, and Zevulun.

Of Jacob's four wives, only Leah was awarded to be buried next to Jacob in the Tom/Cave of the Patriarchs.

Jacob's last two wives were servant maids of Rachel & Leah. His third wife was **Bilhah** who mothered two of the tribes: Dan & Naftali. His fourth wife **Zilfa** who also mothered two of the tribes: Gad & Asher.

ThePower of Words: A Cautionary Tale

In the intricate tapestry of life, one of the most potent yet often underestimated forces are the power of words. Each syllable, phrase, and sentence that escapes our lips carries the potential to shape destinies, mend hearts, and shatter dreams. This truth is vividly illustrated in the story of Rachel, whose unexpected death serves as a poignant reminder of the immense impact that words can wield.

Rachel's untimely passing was not a mere coincidence but a culmination of a series of events set into motion by a chain reaction of spoken words. It began with Jacob's decision to leave the household of his father-in-law, Lavan, taking with him his family and possessions. Lavan, realizing their departure, embarked on a pursuit, intent on reclaiming what he believed was his.

Amid this tense encounter, Rachel, the matriarch known for her profound faith, seized an opportune moment to intervene. In a courageous act of defiance against her father's idolatry, she secretly took Lavan's idols, a move that would unwittingly set forth a cascade of consequences. Her act was a declaration of her unshakable devotion to the one true God, a testament to the power of faith-driven actions.

As Lavan confronted Jacob about the missing idols, a dramatic exchange of words ensued. Jacob, ignorant of Rachel's intervention, passionately proclaimed a curse upon the person responsible for their theft. Little did he know that these uttered words would act as arrows released from his mouth, finding their destination in a most unexpected manner.

The curse struck Rachel, not as a result of any ill intent on Jacob's part, but rather as an unintended consequence of his emotional outburst. This tragic turn of events serves as a sobering lesson in the art of communication. It underscores the need for mindfulness, caution, and profound consideration before giving voice to our thoughts and emotions.

The episode involving Rachel's death resonates with timeless wisdom, reminding us that every word we speak carries weight and consequence. Our words, much like seeds sown into the fertile soil of existence, possess the power to shape our realities, influence others, and ripple across time. Just as the spoken curse unwittingly impacted Rachel's fate, so too can our words bring about unforeseen outcomes in the lives of those around us.

This cautionary tale aligns with the core values of Judaism, which emphasize the sanctity of speech and the importance of ethical conduct. Jewish teachings underscore the significance of speaking words of kindness, empathy, and truth. The concept of "lashon hara," or evil speech, warns against gossip and slander, urging individuals to use their words to uplift and connect rather than to harm.

Matriarchs, their legacies endure as beacons of hope and inspiration

Chapter 5

Jewish Rituals & Routines: Embarking on Spiritual Practices
Morning Wake up

Consider the seemingly ordinary act of waking up each morning.

A moment so often overlooked in its profound significance. Let us

venture into this daily ritual and unveil the layers of its spiritual depth:

In the realm of Jewish philosophy, the body and soul share a dance of intricate connection. As night descends and slumber takes hold, the soul temporarily leaves its bodily vessel, rendering the body an empty shell—a state akin to a "dead" impurity.

The dawn's light ushers in a transformation. The soul rejoins its corporeal partner, rekindling the bond between the intangible and the tangible. Yet, this reunion is not one of simplicity; it is a purification, a sacred rekindling of the divine within.

Before delving into the act of body purification, a profound expression of gratitude graces our lips. As the first rays of consciousness pierce through, we offer thanks to G-Almighty, the living and eternal King, for the return of our soul to its earthly container.

*"I confess before YOU, **G-Almighty, a living and existing King, that you have restored my soul within me, with your great compassion.**"*

How often have we taken for granted the simple act of awakening? Unbeknownst to many of us, each morning G-Almighty bestows upon us a magnificent testament of divine love. The very act of waking up heralds G-Almighty's favor, a decision by the Creator to grant our soul's return to its corporeal vessel.

Consider this: you have awakened today because GOD's love for you knows no bounds. Your soul's return is a testimony to this unceasing love, a daily affirmation that you are cherished beyond measure. Contemplate this notion, and you will uncover that G-Almighty is your unwavering partner in every aspect of your seemingly mundane daily existence.

The soul, an ethereal beacon, shines as a beacon of divine purity. It is in essence the more sacred component of the human composition, whereas the body serves as a vessel to embrace and house this divine essence.

As the soul journeys back to its earthly abode, the body yearns for purification, a cleansing ritual that bridges the connection between the tangible and the divine. Thus, as we embrace the soul's return, we undertake the task of readying our physical vessel to receive this sacred presence.

The Soul Awakening, Ritual of Bonding & its Significance

In this daily awakening, a symphony of spiritual resonance unfolds. With each breath, we acknowledge G-A's boundless compassion and the soul's wondrous return. We recognize that the rhythm of life, the dance of body and soul, is a testament to the divine partnership that accompanies us ceaselessly. And as we embark upon the journey of a new day, we carry with us the knowledge that the ordinary is in fact the extraordinary, and the mundane is infused with the splendor and the glory of the divine.

Methods of Washing hands, Purifying your hands
A Physical Cleansing Ritual for Spiritual Awakening

In the delicate choreography of body and soul, purification emerges as a profound dance, a communion that holds deep spiritual significance:

The soul's exit from the body, a silent departure through the conduit of the fingertips, injects these extremities with an air of sacredness. In reverence to this journey, we embark on the act of purification, understanding that our fingertips are a threshold between the ethereal and the corporeal.

Once one wakes up, a crucial step unfolds; ***Avoid contact with anything, especially other parts of the body, until this sacred cleansing is complete.*** Water becomes our ally, as it aids in this purification process. Using a dual-handled mug, a vessel for this ritual. One grasps the mug with the left hand, and let the waters flow onto your right hand. Then, transferring the mug to the right hand, let the waters cascade onto the left hand and fingertips. This ritual is repeated three times for each hand, a total of six, followed by a gentle drying.

The Body's Symphony: A Marvelous Orchestra of Functions

Pause for a moment to marvel at the miraculous intricacy of our body, the conductor of a symphony of functions. Imagine its astounding ability to sift through the object consumed, retaining the vital and dispelling the harmful. With every morsel and every sip, this wondrous factory operates, discerning between nourishment and waste.

After this symphony, the hands are risen to about the face level, open towards the sky, asking for blessings, while grace prayer is said before the hands are wiped, a prayer of sanctification reverberates:

"Blessed are you, O Lord, our G-d, the King of the world, who sanctified us with his commandments to purify our hands."

In this moment of purification, let us bask in gratitude for the intricate machinery that is our body—a masterpiece sculpted by the Creator's hands. Marvel at the body's innate wisdom to discern, sift, and separate. It is a testament to the divine artistry woven into our very being.

Consider, in awe, our capacity to cleanse and purify, a reflection of the holiness within. Weaving seamlessly between the spiritual and the tangible, we move forward, hands now cleansed, in harmonious resonance with the sacred rhythms that govern our existence.

Embracing Gratitude: A Prayerful Tribute to the Miracle of our Body

In the fabric of existence, our bodies are more than vessels; they are symphonies of intricate design. At the dawn of each day, as we embark on the choreography of life, let us pause to pay homage and gratitude to the wondrous factory that is called *The Human Body*, a marvel sculpted with divine wisdom.

With hearts brimming with reverence, we intone a prayer of gratitude, a hymn to the Creator:

"Blessed are you, O Lord, our G-d, the King of the world, who created man with wisdom. And created in him body parts, pores & hollows. It is obvious and known before your honorable throne that if one of them is closed or if one of them is opened, it will not be possible to survive even for one hour. Blessed are you, O Lord, healer of all flesh and wonders."

This testament to the exquisite orchestration of our being, is not confined to the private realm but extends to every facet of our journey. As we tend to the body's needs and embrace the bodily functions, we invoke this prayer, for within every act lies a symphony of sacred significance.

In the intimate moments after relieving the body, the prayer finds resonance once more. A gesture of acknowledgment to the G-Almighty wisdom that sustains us, we express our gratitude for the body's ability to discern, to filter, and to cleanse. Even in the most mundane of actions, we recognize the sacred, a reminder that the intricate dance of the body is a privilege we cherish and not taken as *GIVEN FACT*.

Let this awareness ripple through every fiber of our existence. Each heartbeat, each breath, a testimony to divine artistry. Our soul, a silent witness, traverses the realms of existence, reporting to the Almighty on our deeds and actions.

In this holistic perspective, we envision angels, emissaries born from our good deeds, an ethereal testament to our actions. Even as we humbly acknowledge our imperfections, we embrace the notion that our virtuous acts send forth celestial guardians to stand by our side, ready to intercede when called upon.

In each dawn's awakening, in every prayer and expression of gratitude, we embrace the miracle of our body and soul. A tapestry of celestial design, woven with wisdom and compassion, reminding us that every breath is a divine melody, every heartbeat a symphonic praise.

Mikveh - Body purification by "Water Immersion"

In the sacred tapestry of Jewish tradition, the concept of purity and impurity finds its embodiment in the waters of the Mikveh—a consecrated pool that offers the transformative power of water immersion.

From the depths of Jewish history, the Mikveh has been a sanctified space, intrinsically linked to purity and spiritual renewal. The need for purification arises from various life occurrences, each necessitating a return to a state of spiritual clarity and holiness.

The archaeological findings of many sites where Jews lived, are reminiscent of many of the Mikveh sites.

Some of the instances that call for Mikveh immersion & purification:

•The first rays of morning sunlight kiss the world awake, and a man rises from his slumber. Before his voice mingles with the chorus of morning prayers, he embarks on a sacred journey to the Mikveh—a ritual that prepares him for the divine dialogue that awaits.

• A woman, her life a symphony of cycles, experiences the rhythm of her own body. From the sacred journey of menstruation to the dawn of renewed purity, the Mikveh becomes her gateway to spiritual reawakening.

• The anticipation of Sabbath's embrace or the heightened devotion of a festival draws men and women alike to the Mikveh's embrace. With hearts and souls attuned, they immerse themselves in waters that symbolize a sacred transition, an unspoken invitation to the Divine presence.

• The intricacies of birth and creation bring forth a unique path of purification. For a woman who has given life to another human being, the Mikveh becomes her bridge between the realms of creation and sanctity, a space where the journey from physical to spiritual is celebrated.

A Mikveh is more than a pool; it is a portal. It beckons the soul to transcendence, inviting it to submerge in the nurturing arms of water, nature's elixir. The source of the water in Mikveh is linked to natural rain or river.

The Mikveh's water imparts a sacredness that cleanses, revitalizes, and elevates the soul & body spiritually.

Importance of Mikveh stands as a testament to the profoundness of sanctification. The construction of a Mikveh precedes the establishment of even a synagogue, highlighting its paramount significance in the life of a Jewish community.

The Mikveh is governed by an intricate web of laws, regulating its preparation, usage, and sanctity. Men and women, adhering to distinct guidelines, approach the Mikveh with a sense of reverence and devotion and holiness prior & after the immersion.

In a world where physical body cleanliness is elevated to a spiritual plane, meticulous care is given to the Mikveh's hygienic maintenance to underscores its holy purpose.

Separated by gender, each Mikveh holds a profound space of spiritual transformation. A sanctuary within a sanctuary, the waters of the Mikveh cradle the seeker, releasing the burdens of impurity and embracing the purity of soul.

In the realm of the Mikveh, the physical and the spiritual merge. The immersion, a sacred gesture, is a metaphorical rebirth, a casting off of impurities and a return to the pristine state of spiritual grace. And as each soul resurfaces from the waters, its journey of renewal echoes through the ages, harmonizing with the whispers of generations past, present, and those yet to come.

A Journey of Renewal, Rejuvenation & Connection

Women's Mikvah
Symphony of Jubilation - Spirit& Body Infusion

The Mikveh process for women is another fascinating event that happens on a rather usual basis. Women after the menstrual period, or after the birthing process are required to use the Mikvah before further martial relations are renewed. Once the woman's body experiences a regeneration for the period of about 7 days, 5-7 number of days are added counting the dry & clean days from blood dissemination before using the Mikveh.

This two-week period, pause and void of marital relationship, allows the body to rejuvenate after the hazardous waste material has been defused through the purification process. The dry days are added to the separation days so that the body can experience the well-deserved resting and refreshing period after the menstrual period insurgency of hormones.

As the physical and spiritual elements couple together to become a woman who cherishes her self-respect and preparedness for feeling close to her husband who has just goosebumps in anticipation of touching her hands after this LONGtwo-week period of abstention of even touching her.

The feeling of the first time touching one another is RENEWED every time she returns from this wonderful adventure of Mikveh submersion.

Observe how G-Almighty's simple commandments (Leviticus 12:1-8) and (Leviticus 15) favor us. How his Omnipresence loves us that gives the women the gift of separation for two weeks to allow the body & spirit rejuvenate.

As she lowers herself into the Mikveh's embrace, an exhilarating rush of water engulfs her, a cascade of renewal that touches not only her body but her very essence. With each ripple, the weight of her journey is lifted, and she offers prayers for herself, her loved ones, and the world. In this intimate encounter, she becomes a conduit for blessings—a vessel of hope and renewal.

Emerging from the Mikveh's waters, a sense of serenity blankets her, a serenity that ignites the spark of connection, intimacy, and love. Imagine her husband, waiting with such a passion to embrace his wife after the two-week abstention, creating an atmosphere of tenderness, dazzling, and joy. As she returns home, the moment is electric, her face has a special glow, reserved for her husband. A rekindling spark of love that first brought them together, a dance of souls and senses.

Of course, the husband in turn prepares the settings with flowers and gifts and a pleasant environment to receive his glorious wife from Mikveh in a fortunate and gratified way. With the belief that G-A has blessed him with his best LIFE SOUL-MATE possible, his ***Eshet Chail***.

Our Grandma's Legacy, A Chilling Mikveh Story:

In a moving & heartbreaking testament to their unwavering commitment, our grandmothers embarked on a remarkable journey that illuminated the depths of their dedication to the sacred commandment of Mikveh. In the face of icy challenges and perilous landscapes, these remarkable women would courageously venture to frozen lakes, where the very act of breaking through ice became a testament to their unyielding faith – Mikveh.

Imagine the scene: a frozen tableau, where winter's chill cast a frosty veil upon the world. Amidst this stark beauty, our grandmothers would brave the bitter cold, driven by a force more potent than the elements. With hearts resolute and spirits aflame, they embarked on a mission of a long trip to the lake that would put their very lives in danger for simply performing G-Almighty's commandment.

In the heart of this frozen terrain, they confronted the icy mantle that veiled the waters beneath. Armed with determination and a deep reverence for tradition, they chipped away at the frozen barrier—a symphony of strength and devotion echoing across the frozen expanse. The cracking ice bore witness to their untamable will, forming pathways to the clear waters below.

Stepping into the frigid pool, their breath suspended in the air, they submerged themselves in an act of profound purification. The icy waters, a metaphor for life's challenges, served as a conduit for spiritual renewal. These fearless women, with their lives hanging in the balance, embraced the Mikveh's embrace, reclaiming a sense of closeness and purity that transcended the physical realm.

Their dedication was not without risk—a risk that underscored the depth of their commitment. They understood that this commandment was more than a ritual; it was a testament to their unwavering love and devotion to their faith. They were willing to brave the cold, to face danger head-on, all in the pursuit of a connection that held immeasurable value. As we reflect on these extraordinary stories, let us remember the extraordinary lengths to which our grandmothers went, the risks they undertook, and the sacrifices they made. Their legacy serves as a powerful reminder of the profound significance of the Mikveh and the unbreakable bonds it strengthens. May their bravery continue to inspire us to embrace our own traditions with the same fervor, commitment, and unwavering love that they exemplified.

This section is dedicated to my grandmother and great grand mother of us all,who delicately, treasured all the Jewish values and traits throughout the tumulus and harsh history from so many generations to our current modern time society, where the traditions and commandments are still being cherished and practiced as they were then.

This book is dedicated to my parents, who left us to the better world 9 years ago, where their burial dates were exactly 40 days apart on the hour! As explained in Chapter 4, "The holiness act of formation of baby", 40 days prior to formation of the baby, a heavenly voice calls for the two souls to be soul-mate for life. This "occurrence", the instance of 40 days separation in the spectrum of their life is not just by accident. It is the attestation to G-Almighty's artful planning and exactness.

Asher Ben Yaacov, 17 Ellul 5774
Miriam Bat Chana, 10 Av 5774

ת.נ.צ.ב.ה.

May their souls rest in peace. Amen

"For a prosperous tomorrow, our past must always remain in our memory."

Chapter 6

Jewish Compassion and Contribution, Impact on the World

The Illuminating Legacy of Jewish Nobel Prize Laureates

The pursuit of knowledge and the advancement of human understanding have been foundational principles deeply embedded in Jewish culture and identity. This commitment to intellectual exploration and innovation is exemplified by the remarkable number of

Jewish Nobel Prize laureates, a testament to the enduring impact of the

Jewish people on the world stage.

The Jewish tradition of valuing education and scholarship traces back thousands of years. The reverence for learning and the exchange of ideas is deeply rooted in ancient texts and teachings, fostering a culture that places a premium on intellectual growth. From the study of the Talmud to the exploration of the natural world, Jewish thought has always been characterized by a deep curiosity and an unwavering dedication to uncovering the mysteries of existence.

Jewish Nobel Prize Winners

Despite being a minority in terms of global population, the Jewish community has contributed significantly to various fields of science, literature, peace, and economics, earning more than its fair share of Nobel Prizes. This remarkable achievement speaks volumes about the indomitable spirit of a people who have surmounted incomprehensible and unconceivable challenges, including the devastating loss of millions during the Holocaust and a long history of persecution and displacement.

The numbers themselves are nothing short of astounding. With a representation of roughly less than 0.2% of the global population, Jews have garnered over 22% of Nobel Prizes across all six categories. This exceptional accomplishment is a testament to the Jewish commitment to excellence, intellectual curiosity, and the relentless pursuit of truth.

The phenomenon of Jewish Nobel Prize winners is not merely a statistical anomaly; it is a reflection of a cultural ethos that revere's education, critical thinking, and the relentless pursuit of bettering the human condition. From groundbreaking advancements in physics, economics and medicine to profound contributions to literature and the promotion of peace, Jewish laureates have consistently demonstrated the potential for individuals to drive monumental change on a global scale.

The connection between Jewish identity and Nobel Prize achievements is not solely coincidental. It is a manifestation of a rich tapestry of history, culture, and resilience. The Jewish experience, marked by challenges and triumphs, has instilled a sense of purpose and determination in successive generations. This collective memory of overcoming adversity has fueled a drive to make meaningful contributions to the betterment of society.

Moreover, the disproportionate number of Jewish Nobel laureates underscores the importance of diversity in shaping the global narrative of progress and innovation. It serves as a powerful reminder that contributions from all corners of the world enrich human's collective understanding and propel us toward new horizons of knowledge.

The exceptional achievements of Jewish Nobel Prize winners illuminate the profound impact of Jewish culture on the global stage. This legacy of intellectual pursuit, resilience, and dedication to the betterment of humanity stands as a testament to the enduring power of knowledge and the transformative potential of individuals who are driven by a sense of purpose greater than themselves. As the torchbearers of peace & enlightenment, Jewish Nobel laureates continue to inspire and guide the world and humanity toward a future defined by progress, compassion, and the unending quest for understanding.

Jewish Compassionate Global Outreach

A Beacon of Hope and Progress

In the intricate web of international relations and global dynamics, Israel and the Jews stand as a testament to the power of empathy, cooperation, and shared progress. Rooted in its intrinsic values of love, respect for humanity, and the sanctity of human rights, Israel's commitment to aiding countries in need transcends borders, cultures, and backgrounds. This compassionate endeavor, driven by a deep-seated belief in the collective right of every individual to thrive, is a shining beacon of hope in a world often marred by challenges.

Israel's approach to international cooperation is grounded in a unique blend of technical expertise and real-world experience. With a history marked by remarkable achievements in areas such as water conservation and irrigation, solar technology, and sustainable development, Israel has become a reservoir of knowledge ready to be shared with those seeking progress. *This sharing of expertise is not driven by a desire for recognition or recommendation; rather, it radiates from a genuine commitment to uplifting fellow nations and fostering a more equitable and better world for ALL humanity.*

One of the most striking examples of Israel and Jews impactful assistance is its pioneering work in water irrigation and solar technology. By harnessing the power of the sun to address water scarcity and agricultural challenges, Israel has offered a lifeline to developing countries, particularly those in Africa plagued by devastating droughts. This transfer of knowledge empowers communities to take charge of their own destiny, enabling them to cultivate life-giving resources and secure a more resilient future.

In a rapidly evolving digital age, connectivity has become synonymous with progress. Israel's dedication to extending the reach of electricity and internet access to even the most remote corners of the globe has transformed communities and opened doors to education, information, and opportunities previously unimaginable. This modernization effort goes beyond infrastructure; it ignites a spark of empowerment, granting individuals the tools to shape their own destinies and participate in the global conversation.

Israel's commitment to international cooperation is a profound embodiment of the values enshrined in its heritage. Just as the Jewish tradition emphasizes the importance of Tikkun Olam, or repairing the world, Israel's actions on the global stage reflect a profound understanding of the interconnectedness of humanity. This interconnectedness forms the basis of a shared destiny, where the progress of one nation reverberates across borders, creating a ripple effect of positive change.

The essence of Israel's compassionate global outreach lies in its recognition that a brighter future for one is a brighter future for all. By offering a helping hand to those in need, Israel showcases the transformative potential of collaboration and mutual support. It demonstrates that progress is not a zero-sum game; rather, it is a collective journey that transcends boundaries and benefits every participant.

Israel's unwavering commitment to aiding and uplifting nations in need is a testament to the power of compassion and cooperation. Through sharing its technical expertise, innovative solutions, and real-world experiences, Israel paves the way for a more just, equitable, and sustainable world. As a beacon of hope and progress, Israel's actions serve as an inspiring reminder of *the profound impact that a small nation with a big heart can have on the global stage.*

Beacon of Light - Israel's Exceptional Leadership Worldwide

Major Disasters and Global Calamities

When calamity strikes and the world is shaken by catastrophic events, one nation stands ready to answer the call of humanity with unwavering resolve and unparalleled expertise. That nation is Israel, a beacon of light and hope in the darkest of times, known for its exceptional leadership and rapid response in the face of worldwide disasters.

In the aftermath of major catastrophes such as earthquakes and avalanches, Israel's elite team of rescue experts' springs into action without hesitation. With a sense of duty and compassion that transcends borders, these professionals board planes bound for the heart of devastation, their mission clear: to save lives, provide relief, and restore hope, while risking their own lives relentlessly.

Take, for instance, the tragic earthquake of February 6, 2023, which struck Turkey and Syria with a magnitude of 7.8, claiming the lives of tens of thousands in a matter of moments. In an astonishing display of efficiency and solidarity, Israel's Search and Rescue teams swiftly reached the disaster-stricken area. Equipped with specially trained personnel, advanced tools, and even rescue dogs, they wasted no time in setting up a makeshift field hospital within 24 hours of the disaster's occurrence!

But the essence of Israel's response goes beyond borders and affiliations. In the face of adversity, Israel offers a helping hand to friend and foe alike, defying conventional norms and political lines. A poignant example lies in Israel's simultaneous offer of disaster assistance to both Turkey and Syria, two countries with complex diplomatic relations. This act of benevolence and compassion underscored Israel's commitment to the shared humanity that unites us all, demonstrating that compassion knows no boundaries.

While Syria's government declined Israel's earthquake assistance officially, Turkey embraced the offer, showcasing the profound impact of Israel's goodwill. The social status, citizenship, or geographic location of those in need became irrelevant in the face of Israel's unwavering commitment to alleviating suffering. Syrians of course unofficially received the same care as residents of Turkey.

The guiding principle was simple yet profound: when a fellow human is in need,

extending a helping hand is the only response.

Israel's dedication to the preservation of life and the betterment of humanity is further exemplified by its consistent role as a frontrunner in disaster response. Among the world's major nations, Israel often stands at the forefront, extending its solidarity, care, and compassion in times of dire need. This leadership role is not just a coincidence; it is a reflection of Israel's deep-rooted values and its people's unwavering commitment to the well-being of all members of the global community.

In a world often divided by political agendas and cultural differences, Israel's remarkable acts of kindness serve as a resounding reminder of our shared humanity. The nation's rapid and compassionate response to worldwide disasters transcends rhetoric and discord, showcasing the boundless potential of unity and cooperation. Israel's legacy as a beacon of hope, love for life, and dedication to the well-being of all resonates far beyond its borders, inspiring us all to rise above adversity and extend a helping hand to those in need.

Israel's Exemplary Leadership in Battle Against COVID19

A Legacy of Hope and Innovation

In the face of the unprecedented and devastating COVID-19 pandemic, Israel once again demonstrated its remarkable resilience and leadership on the global stage. As the world grappled with the sudden onslaught of a formidable foe, Israel emerged as a beacon of hope with the Torch of the Knowledge and a driving force behind groundbreaking solutions that would shape the trajectory of the pandemic response.

At the heart of Israel's exceptional contribution was its unwavering commitment to harnessing cutting-edge advancements in the medical field. The nation's esteemed nucleus of professors, doctors, and intellectuals worked tirelessly to unveil the most advanced and innovative solutions to combat the virus. These dedicated professionals produced a staggering 11% of the scientific reports featured in the renowned New England Journal of Medicine, a testament to Israel's unparalleled intellectual prowess and expertise.

A critical aspect of Israel's resounding success was its ability to conduct comprehensive analyses of the safety and efficacy of vaccines developed by global pharmaceutical giants such as Pfizer, Moderna, and BioNTech. Leveraging an already robust medical network and an extensive database, Israel executed these analyses with precision and depth. The resulting "Highly Cited Papers" not only propelled the medical community's understanding of the vaccines' potential but also illuminated a path forward for the entire world.

Central to Israel's approach was the principle of inclusivity and collaboration. Recognizing the urgency of the situation, Israel made its data and databases readily accessible to pharmaceutical companies, researchers, and individuals alike. This open-door policy underscored Israel's commitment to fostering a collective effort in the fight against COVID-19, transcending geopolitical boundaries and emphasizing the shared responsibility of humanity.

In the true spirit of "leading by example," Israel emerged as the first nation to administer the newly discovered genetically produced vaccine. With unwavering determination and a commitment to precise analysis, Israel meticulously weighed the benefits and potential risks of the vaccine. This information was then shared with major countries and governments around the world, guiding their decision-making processes and steering them toward effective pandemic mitigation strategies.

A cornerstone of Israel's response was its dedication to thorough research and examination of the vaccine's impact on diverse population groups. This rigorous scrutiny extended to pregnant women, children, and infants, reflecting Israel's resolute commitment to ensuring the safety and well-being of all members of society.

Israel's exceptional electronic healthcare system, combined with its status as a global industrial frontrunner, uniquely positioned the nation to rise to the occasion. By seamlessly integrating technology, research, and medical expertise, Israel was able to pierce through the shroud of uncertainty and chaos that enveloped the world. Through its resilience, compassion, and innovative spirit, Israel extended a lifeline of knowledge and expertise to nations far and wide, offering a glimmer of hope and a roadmap to navigate the darkest of times.

Israel's resounding triumph in the face of the COVID-19 pandemic stands as a testament to its invincible & impregnable spirit, unwavering dedication, and boundless capacity for innovation. Through its pioneering research, open collaboration, and unyielding commitment to the welfare of all humanity, Israel illuminated a path forward during a time of unprecedented challenges. As we reflect on this chapter in history, we are reminded of Israel and Jews enduring legacy as a global champion of knowledge, progress, and the collective pursuit of a brighter future.

The Jewish Nation Remarkable Gifts to Humanity

In an era defined by groundbreaking technological advancements, the nation of Israel has consistently emerged as a trailblazer, sharing the fruits of its innovation with the entire world. Israel is a powerhouse of ingenuity and creativity that has bestowed upon humanity some of the most extraordinary 20th & 21st-century technological marvels.

Picture a world connected seamlessly through the marvel of **USB** and **Bluetooth** technology, enabling devices to communicate effortlessly across continents. These modern wonders, integral to our daily lives, are gifts from the brilliant minds of Israel, a nation that understands the power of connectivity and the boundless potential it offers.

Navigating through the maze of modern cities is made easier and more efficient by the gift of **Waze**, a navigation app developed in Israel.

With its real-time traffic updates and crowd-sourced data, Waze has transformed the way we travel, saving time, reducing stress, and making our journeys more enjoyable Worldwide.

Consider the incredible **Sniff Phone**, a revolutionary technology that can detect diseases through the analysis of a person's breath. This life-changing invention holds the promise of early diagnosis and timely intervention, potentially saving countless lives and changing the landscape of healthcare as we know it.

In the realm of mobility and accessibility, Israel's gift of **ReWalk** has transformed the lives of individuals with mobility impairments. This exoskeleton technology empowers individuals to walk again, restoring their independence and dignity in a way that was once thought impossible.

The **PillCam**, another remarkable innovation, has revolutionized medical diagnostics by allowing physicians to visualize the gastrointestinal tract without invasive procedures. This small capsule camera, developed in Israel, offers a non-invasive and patient-friendly alternative, ushering in a new era of medical imaging.

Amid the ever-growing digital landscape, Israel's **Firewall technology** stands as a guardian of cybersecurity, protecting individuals, organizations, and governments from the threats lurking in the virtual world. This gift ensures that our digital interactions remain secure and our sensitive information stays out of harm's way.

The **WaterGen**, an ingenious solution to the global water crisis, has the power to generate clean and safe drinking water from thin AIR. This innovation holds the potential to transform lives in water-scarce regions, offering hope and sustenance to communities in need.

No discussion of Israel's technological contributions would be complete without mentioning **MobilEye**, a pioneer in autonomous driving technology. By pushing the boundaries of innovation, Israel has paved the way for a future where vehicles navigate themselves, enhancing safety, efficiency, and sustainability.

These extraordinary gifts are but a glimpse into the vast and diverse landscape of Israel's technological achievements.

Each innovation represents a labor of love, a manifestation of boundless creativity, and a testament to Israel's unwavering commitment to making the world a better place.

In a world hungry for progress and eager for solutions, Israel's technological gifts shine as beacons of hope with the Torch of Knowledge lid in dark spaces of unknown frontiers and inspiration. These life enhancements technological wonders, remind us of the incredible impact that a small chosen nation, small country, fueled by a spirit of innovation and a desire for global betterment, can have on the entire human race. As we embrace these gifts, we also embrace the boundless potential of the human mind and the infinite possibilities that lie ahead.

Chapter 7

Shabbat, Bride, Queen

Welcome to the HOLIEST day of the week; the 7th day

The fourth of the Ten Commandments that were written on two

tablets that G-Almighty gave to Moses resonates:

"ThyRemember the Day SHABBAT, Keep it HOLY."

In Jewish religion, an official "DAY" starts at sundown until dusk the following day. In keeping with the respect of the Holy day, to make sure that the next regular day has started, an additional 1 hour is added to Shabbat (regularly observed 25 hours). Think of the one-hour time overlap as a Supernatural time zone, that you are still in Shabbat, while officially the next day started.

Although Shabbat has lots, lots, & lots of laws & restrictions on abstention from work or any work-related association, it is a day set aside for *YOU* to relax, delight yourself & family, recharge your batteries for the new week, & exalt your soul.

Shabbat is a day that one can connect spiritually to yourself & your creator. On this rest day that you stop your daily mundane stuff aside, take time to get to know your soul, soul mate & your family members. It is a time to say thanks to G-Almighty on ALL the good he has given us. Although "counting" is considered "work related" and should be abstained on Shabbat; you know what I mean when I say "Count your blessing" even on Shabbat.

Preparation for the Shabbat, Physical & Spiritual

By the entrance of Shabbat, which happens every week at the sunset time, all work-related items MUST stop! In such consideration, every effort is made to be prepared for Shabbat, as soon as possible, as the clock officially hits the sunset for the place one lives, all activities related to the regular week stops;

some of abstention & usage strict restrictions include: phone, internet, tv, radio, traveling, fixing items, planting, turning light on/ off, making/creating things, building, making fire.... It would be fair to add here What you are ALLOWED to do. Any action that is not considered work related or creates new objects.

Of course, as mentioned, there are many laws concerning keeping the Shabbat as correct as possible. At the same time, there are as many exception laws that permit the usage based on the situation. For example, an expected mother in pain, or any issue or concerns that is life threatening takes precedent to the laws of Shabbat, of course the exception laws are explained in depth in the pages of Talmud & Gemara.

The entrance of Shabbat, is sort of like what happens at Times Square in NY once every year at 23:59:59. But for the Jews experience happens every week by Sundown on every Friday night. Oh, What a joy! Believe me. The house cleaning is usually done by Thursday, although there are always some last-minute chores left undone before Shabbat entrance. The dining table is prepared with the best table cover, dishes, glasses, & silverware. All the food is prepared & put on a special large hot plate.

All families prepare for a HOLY day, wearing/ looking the best, as if going to a wedding by welcoming The Bride/The Queen Shabbat to our life. Special seat is set aside for the family provider at the head of table; Two loaves of special breads (Shallot) & Bottle of wine & other drinks are placed on the table. Special candles are usually prepared on crystal candle holders. Of course, the husband does not forget to bring a nice bouquet of flowers for the lady and home.

Ladies Candle Lighting Ceremony (LCLC)

Welcome to one of the most electrifying moments of the week, by lighting the Shabbat Candles. Really think of the moment that new year is announced in Times square by the clock countdown, once a year. Now, multiply it by 52 weeks consistently. A Google search "Official Shabbat Timetable Entrance" can give the <u>precise</u> Shabbat Entrance of every place on earth, by any date, even years ahead of time, which portrays the Jewish super exact precise calendar timetables.

It is the duty of the husband to prepare the candles (of course prior to Shabbat). Usually, a pair of the best possible crystal candle light holders is chosen for this HOLY experience for the lady of the house.

A moment of serenity, being ONE with G-Almighty, ushering the holiness of Shabbat to our homes & lives.

The cornerstone values of the Jewish women's life, is the pursuit of traits of Modesty, Timidness, and Special Shyness, which are reserved for her husband & family only.

At the time of candle lighting, praying the special blessings, she requests & wishes for all these good traits, including the health & wealth for her whole family from G-Almighty for the coming week and days.

The woman and daughters are given the commandment of lighting the two candles, one for KEEPING the Shabbat and the second for REMEMBERING the Shabbat.

By lighting candles, Shabbat officially enters our lives. For the people who experience the Shabbat (as is) with all above mentioned, would never exchange the experience with anything else.

The exhilarating sensation of Shabbat on your body and mind. The impression and perception of fantastic adventure encounters journey with your soul. Enjoying the warm blanket of G-Almighty's grace, compassionate, bountiful, loving, sympathetic, and forgiving around you.

BTW if you were wondering about LCLC, there is no such a thing, sorry! Just thought it is a bit cute, EZ to remember & made it up: Do you like it, Use it: *LCLC*☺

Collective Night Prayers at Synagogue

A synagogue is a place of gathering & assembly for religious worship. Once the candles have been lit, the father & children dress up, clean, shoes polished, hurry & head to synagogues near their home & join many others to accept the Holiness of Shabbat Bride and Queen. As a groom approaches his bride for the first official time. All the prayers are prepared in a very structured way which includes psalms, & some parts directly taken from the Torah. One of the highlights of the Friday night service is the Song Lecha Dodi, which is song by everyone in an unbelievable harmony together. This song was put together around 1548, by Rabbi ShelomoElkabaz, buried in Tzfat.

This collective singing ushers the Shabbat, while the soul spiritually makes the pure bound between the Bride & the Groom. The thrilling, breathtaking moment of the Groom touching the hand of his bride for the first time. The elevation of one's sensations to a higher level unbeknown to him prior to this divine and mystic adventure. Amazing encounters of the soul and body intertwine with JOY of the HOLY day, Shabbat. (Just a reminder: Yes Every Week)

The prayers are recited by the Chazan=Cantor while all congregants are reciting individually and collectively from the Siddur. The usual Shabbat Friday night service takes about an hour in synagogue, staring at the sunset. This collective gathering, and prayers show our commitment to G-Almighty for our belief & feeling secured that G-A is favoring & covering us with all his good thoughts, grace, kind, merci, & compassion ALL the time. Cannot think of a better place to feel the might& power of G-A, where everyone comes together for this beautiful gathering time to say thanks while accepting the Shabbat.

The congregation is called Beit Knesset, also known as a place of gathering. A perfect place to catch up to your friends and relatives whom you might not have seen for some time.

Shalom Aleichem
Pair of Shabbat Angels Escort to our home after Shabbat Eve Services

The synagogue is considered a small temple where you can feel closest to G-A as his majesty's residence, although he is found everywhere. But let us give him the minimum and proper honor to visit his Majesty in his private place.

While approaching the synagogue, one should hurry. Conversely, one must refrain from leaving in a hurry from the synagogue, while heading back home, as two angels follow each person. One of the angles is positive while the second one is not so positive by its nature.

Once reaching home, ***both angels will bless the same blessing:*** "that the home will be the same for the coming week, As Is" while the second angel will say "AMEN". If the home is all prepared, candles lit, the table is set for Shabbat, the angel's blessing will bring harmony for the coming week. Whilst, if the home is not ready for Shabbat, the blessing of the pessimist angel will be in effect.

As soon as returning, everyone stands up by the table and welcome the angels by singing the Song "Shalom Aleichem". There are 5 verses in this song prayed by everyone by the table. They include welcoming the angels by offering or requesting blessings from them:

a. ***Peace be upon you,***
b. ***Come in peace,***
c. ***Grant us your peace***
d. ***Join/Sit with us with peace,***
e. ***May your departure be in peace,*** *(this verse usually omitted as part of respect to Angels, as it could be thought of we are trying to dispel & drive away the Angels"*

Eshet Chail - Let's all praise the wife/mother

Our everyday experiences have sometimes become so routine, that we forget about the complex things that have to happen & work together so that we can live our basic "routine" life. Wake up, breathe, eat, walk, smell, touch, see, hear, ...

This cannot be truer for our home. Let's think for a moment; wife/mother has gone through so much during the week. As the interior minister of the HOME, she has taken care of so much; worked, cleaned, washed, cooked, prepared the children, husband, and hundreds of other chores... Here & there, maybe we say " Thank you" to her, sometimes. Because it has become "So Naturally Routine". She does not even expect or look for our "Thank you or Appreciation ", because she knows well, if she waits for the family's appreciation, the train will squawk and screech to station quickly & everything will

STOP! She keeps on going, as if she has installed in her the best Lithium batteries Duracell has ever produced!

So exactly because we do NOT say enough "thank you" to our wife/mother during the week, we take this weekly opportunity at this beautiful moment, with the presence of Queen Shabbat to show our respect & appreciation to our own home bride & queen.

As such, here is the opportunity for the whole family to *REALLY* say "Thank you" and not just by these (sometimes empty) cliché words. All the family stand up together around the table to *PRAISE* the Wife/mother, as she restfully sits & listens to all the family singing this beautiful ancient poem especially written FOR HER personally and for *ALL WOMEN* collectively.

The poem *"Eshet Chail=Warrior Lady"* was so poetically written by King Solomon, son of King David for his mother, Bat Sheva. It has 22 verses; ALL in the order of Hebrew alphabets. In short we praise and sing together the qualities & values of the lady of the house as such: (Just to name a few:)

- *Her loyalty & caring to husband & family,*
- *Home Economics, Skillfulness, Making & Creating*
- *Wise, Kind-heartedness, Graceful, Thoughtful*
- *Fears G-Almighty; Generosity, Benevolence & Kindness*

Are there other cultures that consistently honor the wife or woman of the household, showering her with well-deserved respect on a regular, often weekly, basis? This practice is not a recent innovation; rather, it stems from ancient traditions and values that have been transmitted through generations and remain integral to Jewish culture. The profound respect accorded to the lady of the house plays a pivotal role in maintaining the cohesion of the family unit.

In Jewish tradition, this concept is deeply ingrained, and it is widely acknowledged that the overall well-being and economic stability of the entire family are intricately linked to the wife's contentment and happiness. This state of contentment is only achievable when both the husband and children extend genuine respect to the wife.

This principle finds resonance in the sixth commandment of the Ten Commandments: "Honor thy father and thy mother." While the commandment does not explicitly mention the wife, it encompasses the broader concept of honoring one's parents, which inherently includes respecting the mother or wife within the household. This commandment serves as a cornerstone of Jewish ethics, emphasizing the significance of showing reverence and appreciation for those who play vital roles within the family structure.

The act of honoring and respecting the wife is not merely a ritual but a profound testament to the importance of nurturing strong family bonds. It acknowledges the invaluable contributions of women in maintaining a harmonious and thriving home life.

In Jewish culture, this practice often takes the form of special rituals and traditions that occur regularly, including the observance of Shabbat, the Jewish day of rest and spiritual rejuvenation. During Shabbat, families come together to celebrate and honor the wife by reciting blessings, sharing meals, and expressing gratitude for her dedication to the household.

Beyond the rituals, the act of respecting the wife is a continuous commitment that extends far beyond weekly observances. It serves as a reminder that building a strong and enduring family structure hinges on recognizing the vital role of the woman in the home.

In essence, the tradition of regularly honoring the wife is a reflection of timeless values and a profound commitment to family cohesion. It demonstrates that within Jewish culture, the respect accorded to the lady of the house is not just a formality but a deeply ingrained and cherished practice that contributes to the well-being of the entire family.

"Honor thy father and thy mother"

BTW: It is STRICTLY forbidden to upset the wife to the point of crying. As her tears today, will be used as testimony & signature of our sins in future, when one day we will eventually have to stand on judgement day in front of G-Almighty defending ourselves shamefully & pointlessly in vain.

So, you want a better economic family status? Simply:

Honor Almighty, Offer Your Gratitude to him for all presents that he has granted you, especially your wife. Be faithful to her; Respect & Love Thy WIFE. & REST Assure!

The Special Wine Blessing
Fusion of Spiritual & Physical

Wine is well known to bring great JOY to a person. It is also an integral & significant part of any Jewish ceremony & celebration. i.e. Shabbat (entrance/farewell), Weddings, Circumcision, Holidays, Passover, Sukkot, Purim, parties and also "Sium Masechet" Ceremony of successfully completing learning one part of Gemara to name a few.

The wine is poured in special cup called "Gaviah"

Some interesting Gematria results; the value of the two words Wine =70 =Secret (**סוד=70=יין**) (Yain=70=Sod). The saying goes where wine enters, the secrets become more obvious.

Judaism strictly prohibits Over Intoxication. The person must show respect for the boundaries which have been set for. The example danger of such irresponsible actions is embossed in our history by "Cham/Ham" incestual encounter with his father, Noah after improper and exaggerated wine usage and the curse he received for disrespecting his father.

Another such punishment is documented in the book of VaYikra, Levictus:16,1. The two sons of Aharon HaCohen, Nadav & Avihoo, were suddenly taken from this world. Talmud & Gemara teach us that this harsh punishment was given to them due to improper usage of wine in the Holy Temple.

Another intriguing event in the history of the Jewish life is the episode incident of 12 Princes of the tribes' Spy Journey prior to entering Israel. As part of the evidence of what they saw in Israel & brought back with them, which has become the EMBLEM of the state of Israel, is a huge grape cluster carried on the shoulders of two persons who supported carrying the pole.

Did you just notice something strange about the EMBLEM? How large was the grape cluster? Two people to carry one brunch? For the answer; Drum please... Each grape was the size of the current chicken egg or larger! Needless to say, what is the destiny of grapes?

All members of the family while standing at the table, usually the husband, or any male members over age of 13 can recite the special wine blessing, who is taking the lead to thank the G-Almighty for this commandment to enjoy the wine that he has provided us through the grapes. Meaning we DO NOT forget even where the wine came from. Which in a way reminds us not to forget our past and vie for a better future all the time.

This might look a bit strange. So many formalities! Who needs this at all? Let's forget all these bureaucracies, open the bottle, drink, and be happy. Who cares about the past? Who knows what will happen in the future? We are here now, let's enjoy, without any consideration to the act of drinking.

Believe it or not, although, all these delays and stops look like extraneous and superfluous activities, they are perfect example of teaching a Jew and the next generation the important traits of patience, respect, and reflection (in this example wine,) on the notion and understanding the spiritual coexistence in everything we do, eat, and drink.

Now here is the partial translation of the blessing, Enjoy the multi-faceted of blessing, Genesis 2,1:

- *It was on the sixth day of creation, Friday. And the heavens and the earth stopped ALL activities.... And G-Almighty rested on the seventh day from his work that he had done the past 6 days and he declared cessation of all work and activities.*
- *G-Almighty blessed the seventh day, because on this Holy day he finished creating nature and all the creatures.*

Holding the cup of wine in the right hand, the leader recites: "*Zavri Maranan = With the permission of all present; May I continue?*"

All the present respond:*L'Chaim = Cheers = Please honor us.* He continues with the prayer:

- *Blessed are you, Lord our G-A, King of the Universe, Creator of the fruit of the vine and grapes:*
- *Blessed are you, Lord our G-A, King of the world. He who has given us the commandment of the Shabbat and chose us to cherish this holy day with love in remembrance of the universe creation process, the beginning of the Holiness and the memory of Exodus from Egypt. You tendered us the offer of Holy Sabbath with love and pleasure. Blessed be you G-A*

for declaring the Shabbat as a Holy Day.

Once done with the blessing, he sips the wine and then passes it on to all present at the table. There are different accepted methods of passing the wine to all, either the same cup of wine passed to all to taste or some of the wine from the cup is disbursed in small cups to all present.

After the tasting of the wine, the children approach the parents to pay proper respect (as complying to *G-Almighty's 6th of the 10 Commandments, Respect Thy Parents*) and kiss their parent's hands, the parents reciprocally will bless each one individually.

The special blessing is the same that Jacob used to bless his children at his last moments of his life. There is a different blessing for:

- *Male*: *May G-Almighty bless you like Efraim & Menashe*
- *Female*: *May G-Almighty bless you like Sarah, Rivka, Rachel & Leah.*

After which each one will receive the following blessing as stated in Numbers :6,22-26.

And the Lord spoke to Moses, saying: Speak to Aaron and his sons, saying: This way to bless the children of Israel, say to them:

- *May the Lord bless you and keep you safe.*
- *The Lord will shine His face upon you and educate you.*
- *May the Lord reveal His face to you and give you peace.*
- *Put my name on the children of Israel, & I will bless them.*

Is one Hungry yet?

Let's Prepare to EAT

Turn off your engines; Here is the official Weekly Holy Thanksgiving Day, "Shabbat", here comes dinner. Enjoy.

Ok, Let's not forget the atmosphere, the wonderful warm room temperature filled with the aroma of all types of food blended together, yet the taste and smell of each one distinctly recognizable separately (fish, chicken, soups, meat) added with the warmth and glimmer shining of candles and more than anything the festive environment, everyone dressed up for a grand celebration event

Now that we have rendered the proper respect for the wine, we can continue with the next item on the agenda; the Bread = Challah. Prior to indulging in the delicious food prepared, we must give proper respect to Bread. The hands are washed with the same type of mug, preferably in the kitchen sink in the following manner: One Fills the mug with the water, holds with the left hand, pours three times on the right hand, then passes the mug to the right hand and pours three times on the left hand. This process is to cleans the hands from the negative forces and vibes. Before wiping the hands, the hands are kept up in front of face (20 cm away) fingers in top direction reciting the following prayer:

"Blessed are you, O Lord, our G-d, the King of the world, who sanctified us with his commandments to purify our hands."

The hands are wiped, approach the table, take a seat, everyone will sit for a few moments quietly, wait for the husband or father to take a seat (again this is as part of paying respect). Once all ready, the father takes two special made breads together in memory of the Holy breads from the temple, and make the following blessing:

"Blessed are you, our G-d, the King of the world, who made possible bread from the earth." - Deep.

Let's take a few seconds to think about this wonderful blessing and its profonde and deep meaning. Amaze yourself with thinking through the process of turning the wheat to bread. Afterwards the bread is cut, dip slightly 3 times in salt, eat from it and pass pieces of bread to everyone present at the table. Just in case, I'm wondering why salt? Why 3 times? Here it is: SALT = מלח(melach) = 40+30+8= 78/3 = 26 (What is so special about 26? = Gematria value of one of G-Almighty's names, which adds up to 26 = "10+5+6+5 =ה+ו+ה+י

"Important"

Due to importance and the holiness of the Omnipresence, it is strictly forbidden to pronounce G-Almighty's name in the above format.The proper format of the pronunciation is reserved for the Cohen Gadol, High Priest in the temple, and only on Yom Kippur.

The acceptable pronunciation for G-Almighty's name, while properly used in blessings, prayers or reading the Torah, Psalms or

other Jewish national heritage such as Gemara, Talmud, are either -"A_oni (missing "d" on purpose) or Elokim.

Any other usage & pronunciation are forbidden.

Now that proper respect is given to bread, the food can be enjoyed. ***"Bon Appetite".*** The first order on the menu is salads & fish. Afterwards, prior to indulging with the meat & chicken, the plate and the utensils used for fish are exchanged for a fresh set of plates & utensils used to enjoy the rest of delicious foods prepared by the queen of the home in honor of Queen Shabbat.

You might rightfully ask about this strange action! Why are the same plates and utensils not reused? Please refer to section KOSHER for further discussion. Now everybody takes his time to enjoy the dinner, no TV, no phones, no work-related material, JUST enjoy the dinner, share thoughts with other members of the family. Learn about the Torah weekly portion. Catch up with each other on how the past week was. The parents can take this time to talk to the children, listen to them on their school activity, their education, their successes, or challenges where the parents can assist them.

During the 4 Shabbat meals, usually songs are song by every member of the family. Sharing of these songs brings a cohesiveness to all present melting the spiritual aspect of Shabbat by whirl winding on all present.

Birkat HaMazon
Thanksgiving Prayer- Grace after EACH Meal

After one enjoys the food, one must not forget to properly appreciate the one who provided him with all the abundance and prosperity.

We are ready to perform the commandment *"You shall eat and you shall be satisfied and Bless the Lord your G-Almighty on the good he has bestowed upon you."* For such preparation, there is another short washing of the fingertips.

Of course, again, I remind you that there are many rules, regulations, customs and traditions on this **commanded blessing**. Presented to you here are just a few of the main ideas in the most simplistic explanations possible.

Birkat HaMazon, Grace After Meal is not exclusive to Shabbat dinner, but **it is said after each meal**(usually) where bread is eaten as part of the meal. The grace after meal is not considered to be an only individualistic prayer, but also collectively acknowledging and giving the proper gratitude to G-Almighty for the Nation of Israel, as well as part of the worldwide population.

Birkat HaMazon, takes about 5-7 minutes reading time from Siddur, it consists of 4 main sections that have been prescribed and appended over the generations. The actual text and precise wording of this prayer is not found directly In Torah. Its text in general mentions the blessings to G-Almighty for providing all the abundance, prosperity and the food for us as well as bestowing the Land of Israel to the people of Israel. Our appreciation is so well deserved because the food and nourishment provided to us by G-A is so crucial to our ongoing living and sustainability, every time, ALL the time.

Exodus 16,1-36, quotes the blessings and all its commentaries and interpretations. Further clarifications can be found in Talmud in the book of "***BLESSINGS***" which includes 68 pages, each Talmud page averages 73,000 words per page!

The miracle of food (מָן = Maan), In the grace after the meal prayer, a Jew remembers, the saga journey of our forefathers bondage and sufferings in Egypt, the miracles they witnessed and experienced in the last year of their slavery, the miracle of 10 plagues on Egyptians ONLY! Miracles as cosmic as you can think of.

The miracles of leaving captivity and slavery. The journey that took 40 years to complete to get to The Holy Land. ***One does not forget the kindness, graciousness, and generosities G-Almighty showed us, by providing the needed water (in merit of Miriam), food (מָן = Maan) (In merit of Moses) or the Clouds (in merit of Aharon HaCohen) which surrounded the Israelites in all 6 directions, during their journey in desert for 40 years, up to the point that they did not even need to change shoes.***

Take a quick minute to think to grasp the magnitude of 600,000-man, and their families, wandering in the desert for 40 years. The grand responsibility of well-being of every one during this long journey to provide for the water, food, and encapsulation everyone in make-shift dueling clouds.

It is our responsibility to properly acknowledge by thanking the G-Almighty for handling the operation in such a galactical magnitude, single-handedly with flying colors, even if it was over 3000 years ago. For if it was not in His Majesty's favor, we would still be living in slavery and bondage in Egypt.

Maan, a super-natural item that would every night pour and rain down to earth is documented as looking like a wafer. In the morning, the people would go outside and gather these wafers. Their taste? What they wished for! Whatever their taste buds fancied. Amazing! They were supposed to take as much as they needed for all family members. Any extra or left over Maan would be spoiled and non-usable.

Guess what, the miracle of Maan pouring from heavens would cease on Shabbat. Instead on Fridays, they would pour double the regular daily portion to cover the whole Israelite Nation food for 2 days in a row!

Think of logistics issues surrounding providing food for at least 600,000 (Man over age of 18) & their families in the desert, (heat of the day, brutal chill of the nights) even with today's most modern technological facilities and transportation for a full 40 years continuously. Nonstop!

This prayer, like many other prayers, are not individualistic, but rather have in mind all our Jewish and non-Jewish brethren's. Such is this prayer, that we thank G-A for saving us from Egypt slavery and we wish that slavery and famine will NOT be witnessed or experienced anywhere in the World.

The prayer continues to thank and wish for peace, health, wealth, that no one should starve.

So, what do you say? Is Thanksgiving Day an annual event which happens only on the last Thursday of November each year?

We must be thankful for our being and having what we have, appreciate our health, be grateful for G-Almighty who blesses us every day and every minute.

May the teachings of this book and specifically this section lighten the readers eyes to see the spirit in you. Be thankful to G-Almighty for all you have, appreciate what you are. Recognize the spiritual aspect of all mundane everyday living.

Let us count our blessings

Let us give proper thanks to the Almighty who has bestowed so much good upon us.

Let us always look at the half glass full, Not the empty half.

Let us respect the teachings of the Torah in our daily lives.

The Spiritual Significance of Shabbat
A Journey of Rest, Learning, and Connection

Shabbat, the seventh day of the Jewish week, is a cherished time of spiritual renewal, rejuvenation, reflection, and connection with the Divine. It is a day that begins with morning services, a time of communal prayer, and Torah portion readings that set the tone for a day of rest, relaxation, and deepening one's relationship with God. Here we will explore the various aspects of Shabbat during the day, including morning services, Torah learning, festive meals, and the spiritual journey that unfolds, allowing individuals to draw closer to the Almighty.

Morning Services and Torah Portion Readings

Shabbat morning services hold a central place in the observance of this holy day. The congregation gathers in synagogues to engage in communal prayers, singing, uttering hymns of praise, and connecting with the Divine presence. These services are a vital time for worship and reflection, as well as an opportunity to come together as a community to strengthen their shared bond.

One of the highlights of the morning services is the reading of the weekly Torah portion, which has been set in advance to complete the whole Torah during the year. Torah is not considered just another book! The significance of Torah is far reaching than what our limited mind can imagine. Once the Torah portion for the weeks throughout the year comes to an end, this book is not put aside as "I am done reading it." It is believed that there are 70 facets, aspects, and dimensions to Torah. So once completed ALL the Torah portions, again we continue at the Beginning, the Genesis 1:1. Think of it as a back to the drawing board to find additional components, features, hidden messages of Torah that one possibly has missed. Correction: Most definitely missed priorly.

The final portion of the Torah reading is from the book of Deuteronomy 33.1 read on the Holiday of Simchat Torah (The Joy of

Torah.) This exhilarating Holy day has its own merit by itself, which falls day after 7 days of Sukkot Holiday, the feast of tabernacle. The Holiday of Simchat Torah show the continuance & our profound bondage with the G-Almighty, on this Holy day filled with unimaginable jubilation, after completion of all Torah weekly reading, we continue reading the Torah (from another set) right away from the beginning of Torah Genesis 1.1. "We are never done!" Let's forge ahead.

During the Shabbat AM prayer, the weekly Torah portion is read by a designated Torah reader aloud from the sacred text, Torah Parchment. The significance of the weekly portion is expounded upon by the Rav or other members of the community. The Torah portion is a source of guidance, wisdom, and moral lessons, inviting individuals to reflect on its teachings and apply them to their lives. It serves as a foundation for the day's spiritual journey, providing a framework for deeper understanding and growth.

Relaxation and Learning: Balancing Rest and Spiritual Enrichment

Shabbat is a day of dual significance - a day of rest and a day of spiritual enrichment. It is a time to step away from the hustle and bustle of the workweek, to pause and recharge. ***The concept of "rest" in Judaism is not merely about physical relaxation, but also a state of mental tranquility and spiritual elevation. The cessation of labor on Shabbat creates an opportunity for individuals to redirect their focus towards matters of the soul and spirituality to engage in activities that cultivates one's inner peace.***

At the same time, Shabbat encourages the pursuit of knowledge and learning. While the day is marked by rest, it is not a passive idleness but an active engagement with the Torah and its teachings. The interplay between relaxation and learning on Shabbat amongst the family creates a harmonious balance, allowing individuals to nourish their minds, hearts, and spirits.

Festive Meals and Spiritual Nourishment

The observance of Shabbat extends to the culinary realm as well, as it is customary to enjoy festive meals that are imbued with intention and meaning. The Friday night meal, known as the "Shabbat dinner," and the Shabbat day meals are occasions to celebrate the gift of sustenance and togetherness. These meals often begin with the recitation of blessings over bread and wine, acknowledging G-Almighty's role as the ultimate provider.

The Spiritual Journey of Shabbat: Drawing Closer to the Divine

Shabbat provides a day of journey of the soul towards a deeper connection with the Divine. The combination of communal prayer, Torah study, rest, and fellowship creates an environment conducive to spiritual growth. As individuals immerse themselves in prayer and study, they transcend the material concerns of everyday life and engage in a dialogue with the Almighty. As individuals engage in these practices, they draw closer to the Divine presence, cultivating a deeper understanding of themselves, their faith, and their relationship with the Almighty.

The rhythm of Shabbat, punctuated by prayer services and moments of contemplation, serves as a reminder of the sacredness of time. It provides an opportunity to step out of the chronological stream and enter a space where the temporal and the eternal intersect. This day offers a taste of the harmony and peace that will characterize the Moshiach era, where all humanity will come to recognize and acknowledge the Divine presence.

Havdalah
A Multisensory Journey of Spiritual Upliftment

Havdalah, is a beautiful ceremony that marks the end of Shabbat and the beginning of a new week. It is a powerful experience that engages multiple senses, creating a unique spiritual journey. Through sight, taste, touch, and smell, Havdalah transcends the ordinary and elevates the soul, fostering a connection to the Divine and a renewed sense of purpose. After 25 hours of Shabbat who engulfed us with unbelievably spiritual uplifting, we start to feel the sadness of the vacuum that it leaves behind. Leaving us to again face the challenges of the mundane weekly tasks, chores again.

In an effort to sustain the exhilarating feeling of Shabbat as much as possible, the gift of Havdalah (set aside, separate, distinction) is bestowed upon Jews, where all senses are put to exercise. Proper prayer is said on each of the parts of this beautiful ceremony listed below:

Sight: The Flame of Transition

At the heart of the Havdalah ceremony is the glowing flame of the braided candle. As the sun sets and darkness enters, this candle's flame pierces the obscurity, symbolizing the transition from the sanctity of Shabbat to the opportunities of the week ahead. The dancing flame draws the eye, captivating our attention and representing the light that accompanies us through both literal and metaphorical darkness. In this visual transition, we find a reminder that even in moments of challenges, G-Almighty's guiding presence illuminates our path.

Taste: The Sweetness of Separation

The tasting of sweet wine or grape juice during Havdalah is a sensorial contrast to the bitterness of parting with Shabbat. The transition from the sweetness of rest to the challenges of the week is a profound reminder of life's duality. As we savor the sweetness on our lips, we recognize the beauty in both our taste buds & the serene scene of the spirit within. This taste serves as a lesson that every experience, be it bitter or sweet, is a part of a greater G-Almighty's grandiose plan.

Touch: Bridging the Gap

The sensation of touching the mint or myrtle branches to bring out the fascinating smell is a nourishment for the Soul, by elevating the spirit even more to approach and get closer to the Omnipresence.

The act of touching the branches to separate the smell from the physical branch reminds us that there is more to what meets the eye. The smell of the branch in a way is considered to be the higher level of being in the branch as perhaps the soul & spirit of the branch which comes out only if you touch it.

My mother, blessed by her memory, would say: "Woman is like mint or myrtle, until you won't touch them, the beautiful smell would not come out." This was a teaching on how one must treat his wife, with love, love & more love.

Smell: A Fragrance of Hope

The mint, myrtle branches or other fragrant spices used in Havdalah elevate the senses of the smell. The aromatic spices represent the beauty hidden within challenges, much like the fragrance concealed within the rough exterior of the spices. Inhaling these scents encourages us to seek the hidden blessings in the days ahead, even if they are not immediately apparent. The intertwining of scent and spirituality prompts us to embrace hope and optimism, even when faced with uncertainty.

Seudah Revieit: A Gathering of Gratitude

Following the Havdalah ceremony, many people partake in a "Seudah Revieit," another festive meal marking the continuation of Shabbat's spirit. Usually simpler meals are chosen, to emphasize our gratitude, as we express thankfulness for the blessings we have received. In sharing food, stories, and companionship, we acknowledge the gift of nourishment and the importance of community. The Seudah Revieit becomes a reminder that the blessings of Shabbat extend beyond its formal observance, lingering in the moments of togetherness we share.

Havdalah is a sensory-rich experience that encapsulates the essence of transition, renewal, and gratitude. Through sight, taste, touch, and smell, this ceremony bridges the gap between the holy and the everyday, fostering a profound connection to the Divine and to the world around us. As we engage our senses in the Havdalah ritual and partake in the Seudah Revieit, we are reminded that even as Shabbat comes to a close, its spiritual upliftment continues to infuse our lives, guiding us through the challenges and joys of the week ahead.

"The key to a radiant future lies in the preservation of our past."

Chapter 8

Kosher Lifestyle: Nurturing Body Mind and Spirit

Where do I begin?

Kashrut, the intricate system of Jewish dietary laws, is far more than a set of rules governing what one can and cannot eat. It is a profound practice that encompasses the physical, ethical, and spiritual dimensions of nourishment. Rooted in ancient traditions and deeply woven into Jewish culture, Kashrut is a testament to the interconnectedness of humanity, Divine, and the world. I will try to shed some light on the multifaceted nature of Kashrut, its origins, significance, and its impact on well-being.

In general, wild animals, hunted animals, animals with specific physical attributes such as the animal with split hoof, camel, rabbit, pig, giraffe, rodents or multi-digestion system are strictly prohibited.

Tamed and controlled animals (with no injuries) such as cow, sheep are generally allowed, with proper preparation after humane and merciful slaughtering of the creature that G-Almighty has blessed us with.

Strict rules ensure the animal would feel the least amount of pain prior to the spirit of the animal leaving the physical arena after Schechita. The knife, used by Shochet (the person) has strict, stringent rules & guidelines. Its sharpness and accuracy are at most and regularly checked to ensure a humane shechita(butchering) of the tame animals for our daily sustenance.

The next class of animals are birds. Again, wild feathered flying animals such as Eagle, vulture are strictly prohibited. On the other hand, domestic healthy birds such as chickens, & ducks are allowed, again after the proper preparation ....

Of course, we cannot forget about the exquisite class of nutritional food: The family of creatures G-A created who have to live in water as their natural environment. The ***ONLY TYPE of FISH*** allowed in Judaism are the ones that have ***TWO*** distinct signs: Scale & Flipper such as white fish, Cod, Salmon. By the way, if only one sign exists in the fish, it does not qualify. All others sea living animals and creatures, Sorry! Just think of their living surroundings and the food they consume for their sustainment! One would not need the nourishment that its origins base are not satisfying to one's eyes, or tastebuds.

Do you see the trend? No wild or ferocious animals, no hunted animals, ONLY the tamed, domesticated living in a relatively clean and calm normal environment. The Food that these animals consume. It should not be at a higher spiritual level of the animal himself. And of course, so much so, that their food should ***NOT*** be at such a level in the food chain ladder (such as pigs feed. I am sure I do not need to explain or expand about their living room and manners.) And WHY you may ask? ***What is all the fuss about?***

The Foundation of Kashrut

At the heart of Kashrut lies a set of principles and guidelines that dictate the permissible and forbidden aspects of food consumption. These laws, derived from the Torah, categorize animals, birds, and aquatic creatures into distinct groups. While the specifics are vast and intricate, the underlying theme is clear: Kashrut promotes the consumption of animals that are considered pure, domesticated, and morally raised, while forbidding the consumption of animals that are wild, ferocious, or display specific physical attributes.

Mindful Consumption and Ethical Choices

Kashrut encourages a heightened awareness of the choices we make when it comes to nourishing our bodies. By abstaining from certain animals and ensuring that those consumed are prepared in a humane and respectful manner, individuals become mindful stewards of creation. The act of eating becomes an ethical practice, emphasizing compassion for animals and an acknowledgment of the sanctity of life. This mindfulness extends beyond the plate and influences one's interactions with the world at large. The consciousness of the origins of any food we consume, be it bread, fish, chicken or meat. The understanding that what we eat, was created for this purpose meticulously by the grand plans of G-Almighty.

The Separation of Dairy and Meat

The phrase "לא תבשל גדי בחלב אמו" (Lo Tevashel Gedi B'Chalav Imo) is mentioned three times in the Torah. This command appears in the following verses:

1. Exodus 23:19: "You shall not cook a young goat in its mother's milk."
2. Exodus 34:26: "You shall bring the first of the first fruits of your ground to the house of the LORD your God. You shall not boil a young goat in its mother's milk."
3. Deuteronomy 14:21: "You shall not eat anything that has died naturally. Give it to the foreigner residing in your town, and they may eat it, or sell it to a foreigner. Because you are Holy People to G-Almighty. Do not cook a young goat in its mother's milk."

In each of these verses, the Torah prohibits the cooking of a young goat in its mother's milk. This command is the basis from which the interpretation of not mixing meat and dairy products is derived in Jewish dietary laws, known as **Kashrut**. It is a foundational principle that is examined in the context of the Torah, and it is one of the laws governing kosher ovens (or pots) and dishes in Jewish tradition, especially in regard to the prohibition of cooking a mixture of meat and dairy.

By conforming to the Kashrut laws as listed above, one can internalize the possible deep-rooted reason for these sometimes stringent laws. Please consider the compassion and the sensitivity towards the calf & her mother being prepared together. Ask yourself, "Would this not be considered as an arrogant, egoistic and self-centered act." *All of a sudden, things look a bit different.The spiritual aspects of eating sprout blossoming and shed new light on what we consume for our sustainment.*

Physical Well-being and Holistic Health

While Kashrut was established long, long time before modern food safety practices, many if not most of its guidelines align with today's contemporary health recommendations. The meticulous attention to food preparation, the prohibition of consuming blood, and the avoidance of certain animals contribute to a reduced risk of foodborne illnesses. By adhering to Kashrut, individuals prioritize their physical health and well-being, aligning with the Jewish belief in caring for the body, a vessel for the Divine spark.

Spiritual Elevation Through Nourishment

Kashrut transforms eating into a sacred act, elevating it to a spiritual level. The intentional separation of dairy and meat, the blessings recited before and after meals, and the conscious choices made about sourcing and preparation all contribute to a profound sense of gratitude and mindfulness. Kashrut is a reminder that every meal is an opportunity for connection, with oneself, others, and the

Divine. Through this practice, individuals cultivate a deeper relationship with their inner selves and the world around them.

Kashrut in Israel: A Holistic Experience

In Israel, the practice of Kashrut extends beyond individual households to encompass various aspects of society, including hospitality and tourism. Many hotels' adherence to the laws of Kashrut exemplify a commitment to providing guests with not only physical sustenance but also spiritual fulfillment. These establishments ensure that every meal aligns with the principles of Kashrut, inviting visitors to partake in a harmonious blend of Jewish tradition, culinary excellence, and holistic well-being.

Kashrut is a comprehensive practice that bridges the gap between the material and the spiritual, the mundane and the sacred. It is a journey of mindful consumption, ethical choices, and spiritual elevation. Through the observance of Kashrut, individuals transform their meals into moments of connection, gratitude, and Divine presence. As Jews embrace the practice of Kashrut, we honor our heritage, while nourishing our bodies, we elevate our souls, fostering a deep and enduring relationship with the teachings of the Torah and the profound bond with the Omnipresent.

The Culinary Tapestry of Israel: "Kibbutz Galiot Effect"
A Journey Through Jewish Food from the World

"Kibbutz Galiot" refers to the gathering of Jews from all over the world in Israel, which is a visionary event by the coming of Mashiach. Perhaps if we look at the events that have occurred and continue to happen from a bird's eye view over the last century, we can exclaim that we experience living in a Mashiach era, where Jews from all over the world gather in Israel.

Jews over the past century from around the world, have made "Aliyah"=(Rise, or Increase in Spirituality). Some have chosen Israel as the preferred place to live in the world for the enhanced standard of living environment, compare even to the comfort zone of some of the Best Western "Democratic Countries" they resided previously.

And yet there are so many Jews are forced to leave everything behind and make a mass immigration. Israel has been a beacon of hope as a light tower in the vast ocean of helplessness. Usually, antisemitism behaviors of their host countries have forced Jews to emigrate starting from WW1 from Russia & Europe.

The atrocities & horrors of the Holocaust led to the loss of millions of Jewish lives all over in Europe. Survivors and refugees sought refuge in Israel, contributing to a major wave of immigration after World War II.

Next waves included Jews living in middle eastern predominantly Moslem countries in the 1950's to current. To name a few Iran, Iraq,

Syria, Egypt, Morocco and as recently as 2022/23, the mass immigration of Jews from Ukraine.

The Impact of Global Immigration on Israeli Cuisine:

The influx of Jews from diverse cultural and culinary backgrounds to Israel has significantly enriched Israeli cuisine. These immigrants brought with them a wide array of flavors, ingredients, and cooking techniques, contributing to the multicultural tapestry of Israeli food.

Culinary Diversity

Jews from different parts of the world, including Europe, North Africa, the Middle East, and the Americas, brought their unique culinary traditions to Israel. This diversity is reflected in the multitude of dishes and flavors found in Israeli cuisine.

For example, Ashkenazi Jews from Eastern and Central Europe introduced dishes like gefilte fish, matzo ball soup, and latkes, which have become part of Israeli Jewish culinary heritage. Sephardic Jews from Spain, North Africa, and the Middle East brought their own delicacies, such as shakshuka, couscous, & various kebabs.

Fusion Cuisine:

The melding of culinary traditions from different regions and cultures has given rise to fusion cuisine in Israel. Chefs and home cooks often experiment with combining ingredients and techniques from various backgrounds, resulting in innovative and delicious dishes.

Influence on Street Food:

The influence of global immigration can be seen prominently in Israeli street food. Street vendors across Israel offer a wide variety of dishes inspired by international flavors. For instance, the beloved Sabich, a pita sandwich filled with fried eggplant, hard-boiled eggs, and tahini, reflects the fusion of Iraqi & Jewish cuisines.

Culinary Celebrations:

Israeli culinary festivals and events often showcase the diverse food traditions brought by immigrants. These gatherings provide an opportunity for Israelis and visitors to sample dishes from different regions and learn about the cultural significance of each dish.

Israel, is often referred to as the "Land of Milk and Honey," boasts a diverse and delectable culinary scene. Its cuisine is a harmonious blend of Jewish, Middle Eastern, and Persian influences, reflecting the rich tapestry of cultures and traditions that have converged in this historic land. From the bustling markets of Tel Aviv to the aromatic kitchens of Jerusalem's Old City, Israel's food offerings are as varied as its people. Here are a few for your taste buds:

Falafel and Hummus: Middle Eastern

Falafel, the beloved deep-fried balls made from ground chickpeas or fava beans, originated in the Middle East and is an integral part of Israeli street food culture. Served in pita bread with tahini sauce, salad, and pickles, falafel is a savory delight, crispy on the outside and tender on the inside.

Hummus, another Middle Eastern favorite, is a creamy spread made from chickpeas blended with tahini, olive oil, lemon juice, and garlic. It's often drizzled with olive oil and sprinkled with paprika or sumac. The versatility of hummus makes it a staple on Israeli tables, whether as a dip, sandwich spread, or accompaniment to grilled meats.

Shawarma: The Meaty Treat

Shawarma, succulent slices of marinated meat (usually lamb, chicken, or beef), are roasted on a vertical rotisserie and served in a pita or laffa (a larger flatbread). Accompanied by tahini, vegetables, and pickles, this savory and juicy dish is a Middle Eastern favorite.

Shakshuka: A Hearty Breakfast Dish

Shakshuka, originally from North Africa, has become an Israeli breakfast classic. It features poached eggs in a rich tomato and pepper sauce, spiced with paprika, cumin, and chili peppers. Served with crusty bread, this dish is a comforting and spicy start to the day.

Jewish Delicacies: Sephardic Influences

Sephardic cuisine adds a vibrant Mediterranean flair to Israeli food. Dishes like sabich (stuffed pita with fried eggplant and hard-boiled eggs), sambusak (savory pastries), and malabi (a rosewater-flavored pudding) reflect the rich culinary heritage of Sephardic Jews.

Persian Influences: Aromatic and Exotic

Persian Jewish immigrants have brought their unique exquisite culinary traditions to Israel. Some of the popular Persian dishes include Gondi (chicken or meat dumplings),variety of stews like Khoresht: (Sabzi, Karafs, Bademjan, Fesenjan (a usually sweet pomegranate and walnut stew), and of course variety of types of rice known as Polo or ChelloBaghali polo (rice with dill and beans).

Let's not forget the Zaffran, the most favorable fragrant spice used in Persian dishes brings your senses to a new dimension. And how can one forget the Tah-Dig, fried rice at the bottom of the pot which shows up on the top as the pot of rice is reversed in a tray. Site to see!

The combination of fragrant spices, herbs, and full table presentation of Persian cuisine adds a delightful dimension to Israel's culinary landscape.

Street Food Delights

Israeli street food is an experience in itself. From Sabich and shawarma to Malabi and Knafeh (a sweet pastry dessert), the streets are filled with vendors offering a diverse array of flavors and textures. The accessibility of these foods makes them a favorite among locals and tourists alike.

The Fusion of Flavors

Israel's culinary scene is not just about tradition; it's also about innovation and fusion. Chefs in Tel Aviv, often referred to as the "food capital of world," experiment with flavors from around the world, creating a unique blend of global and local cuisine. Whether it's seafood restaurants overlooking the Mediterranean or hip cafes serving artisanal coffee and pastries, Israel's culinary creativity knows no bounds.

Israeli cuisine is a reflection of the country's vibrant history and diverse population. It's a testament to the power of food to bring people together, transcending borders and backgrounds. From the iconic falafel and hummus to the exotic flavors of Persian dishes, Israel's culinary scene is a feast for the senses, inviting visitors to savor the rich, complex, and delicious tapestry of flavors that make up this remarkable nation's cuisine.

Kashrut-Culinary Ethics and Cultural Identity

The Secrets of Jewish Dietary Prohibition

The prohibition against cooking a young goat (or any meat) in its mother's milk is rooted in a far sighted spiritual realm, which is interpreted and elaborated upon in Jewish tradition. While the exact reasons for this prohibition are not explicitly stated in the biblical text, rabbinic literature and commentary offer several explanations and insights:

Avoiding Cruelty and Insensitivity: One common interpretation is that the prohibition serves as a reminder of compassion and sensitivity towards animals. Cooking a young animal in its mother's milk might be seen as a cruel and insensitive act, as it symbolizes taking advantage of the maternal relationship in a way that lacks respect for the natural order and the bond between parent and offspring.

Separation of Life and Death: Another interpretation is that the prohibition emphasizes the separation of life and death. Mixing the milk of a living creature, which represents nurturing and life, with the flesh of a slaughtered animal, which represents death, could be seen as a violation of this fundamental distinction. *By avoiding such mixture consumption, individuals protect their bodies and mind from such internal conflicts, adding to the harmony they bring to their lives and others by becoming aware of the additional unmaterialistic aspect of the food consumed..*

Avoiding Pagan Practices: In ancient Near Eastern cultures, there were instances of cooking meat in milk as part of ritualistic practices. Some scholars suggest that the prohibition might have been introduced to distinguish the dietary practices of the Israelites from those of neighboring pagan cultures. By refraining from cooking meat and milk together, the Israelites would be setting themselves apart and avoiding associations with foreign religious rituals.

Symbolic Holiness and Purity: The combination of meat and milk might be seen as a mixing of opposites, as they come from different realms of existence (animal life and sustenance). The prohibition could thus symbolize the concept of holiness and purity through separation. By adhering to this prohibition, individuals are reminded of their commitment to maintaining spiritual and ethical boundaries.

Preservation of Identity and Memory: The prohibition may also serve as a means of preserving the distinct identity of the Jewish people and their commitment to following the commandments of the Torah. By adhering to dietary laws such as the prohibition against cooking meat and milk, individuals maintain a visible and tangible connection to their heritage and history.

It's important to note that these explanations are based on interpretations and teachings within Jewish tradition, and different sources may emphasize various aspects of the prohibition. The exact reasons for this commandment may remain open to interpretation, but the prohibition continues to be an integral part of kosher dietary practices for many Jewish communities.

From Limitation to Liberation
Unveiling the Spiritual Depths of Shabbat's Prohibited Tasks

There are 39 Melachot or tasks that are forbidden on Shabbat. The concept of observing the Shabbat, is deeply rooted in Jewish tradition and involves refraining from certain activities to honor the sanctity of the day. One of the key principles of Shabbat observance is the prohibition of performing specific types of work related, known as the "39 Melachot." These 39 categories of activities are based on the types of work that were required for the construction of the Tabernacle in the wilderness, as described in the Torah.

The 39 Melachot encompass a wide range of actions, and the list serves as a guide to help individuals understand what is prohibited on Shabbat.

It's important to note that these categories cover a broad range of activities, and specific rules and interpretations may vary among different Jewish communities and traditions. Observant Jews study these laws and guidelines to understand how to uphold the sanctity of Shabbat while refraining from the prohibited activities.

To a new eye, it might look that with so many restrictions in keeping in adherence with Shabbat and Kashrut between so many more laws., What is left to do on Shabbat? However, the beauty of Shabbat lies not in what is prohibited, but in the profound spiritual and transformative opportunities it offers.

Shabbat is a time of rest,renewal, and connection—both with oneself and with the world around. By refraining from these specific creative activities, individuals create a sacred space for deeper connections, reflection, and spiritual growth. Of course in addition to allowed tasks such as accepting the queen Shabbat, eating, drinking (both to acceptable limits), singing, reading, ...

Let's explore the spiritual connections that arise from the limitations of the 39 Melachot and how they enrich one's relationship with family, nature, and oneself:

Closer Family Connection: With the focus shifted away from labor-intensive tasks, Shabbat becomes an opportunity for quality time with family. The absence of work-related distractions allows for meaningful conversations, shared meals, and bonding moments that nurture relationships. Through the observance of Shabbat, families can strengthen their emotional ties, create lasting memories, and cultivate a sense of unity and support.

Explore Nature and Creation: The limitations on creative tasks on Shabbat encourage a heightened awareness of the natural world. People are free to step outside, walk and admire the beauty of nature, while marveling at the divine creations. The act of slowing down and observing the environment fosters a deep connection to the world around us, reminding us of our role as stewards of the Earth. Shabbat becomes a day to appreciate the wonders of creation and practice gratitude for the abundance provided.

Appreciate Spiritual Reflection: Shabbat offers a unique opportunity for spiritual contemplation and introspection. Freed from the demands of work, individuals can engage in prayer, meditation, and study. The absence of worldly distractions creates an atmosphere conducive to inner growth, self-discovery, and a strengthened connection to the Divine. The limitations of the Melachot encourage a focus on the inner journey and spiritual development.

Indulge in Creative Expression and speech: While the 39 Melachot restrict certain creative activities, they also encourage alternative forms of creative expression. Individuals are free to engage in activities such as studying &teaching, Torah, singing, storytelling, and artistic endeavors that bring joy and inspiration without violating the prohibitions. Shabbat becomes a canvas for exploring one's creative talents and fostering a sense of fulfillment and satisfaction.

Rest and Renewal: Shabbat's emphasis on rest is not merely physical; it extends to mental and emotional well-being. By refraining from work-related stresses, individuals experience a profound sense of rejuvenation. This restorative quality of Shabbat allows people to recharge their energy, reduce anxiety, and approach the new week with a fresh perspective.

In essence, the restrictions of the 39 Melachot serve as a framework for embracing the spiritual essence of Shabbat. By setting aside these specific tasks, individuals open themselves to deeper connections, with family, nature, their inner selves, and ultimately, the Divine. Shabbat becomes a sanctuary of peace, a time to celebrate the beauty of existence, and an opportunity to engage in activities that nourish the soul. As the sun sets on Friday evening, the limitations of the Melachot usher in a sacred space of rest, reflection, and renewal that transcends the material world and invites individuals to experience the profound richness of the spiritual realm.

Chapter 9

Mishkan

Temples & Ancient Sacred Spaces: Connecting The Earth & Heavens

Jerusalem; The Spiritual Epicenters of Judaism, the Holiest place in the universe. Jews all over the world use their compasses in directing their prayers towards Jerusalem and within Jerusalem, what is at this point, the remains of the two holy temples that were destroyed almost completely.

The Mishkan, meaning "dwelling place," was a portable sanctuary that accompanied the Israelites during their journey in the desert. It was a physical manifestation of G-Almighty's presence among His people. Constructed with utmost care and precision, the Mishkan contained sacred items such as the Ark of the Covenant and the menorah. It represented a hub of communal worship, where offerings were made, rituals performed, and a connection between the Divine and the human was fostered.

Throughout Jewish history, there have been significant centers of worship that hold deep spiritual and cultural significance. These places of worship, all have played a vital role in shaping the religious identity and practices of the Jewish people. *Glory, Fame, Radiance, & Splendor of Sacred Spaces of Worship, the Mishkan, the First and Second Temples are ALL etched in DNA memory of each Jew.*

The First Temples

The First Temple, also known as Solomon's Temple, was a monumental structure built in Jerusalem. It was a symbol of the united Israelite monarchy and served as the central place of worship for several centuries. *The First Temple was renowned for its architectural grandeur and the presence of the Ark of the Covenant. It became a spiritual epicenter where sacrifices were offered, festivals celebrated, and the Israelites' relationship with God was strengthened.*

However, the First Temple was eventually destroyed by the Babylonians in 586 BCE, leading to a period of exile. The Second Temple, built after the Babylonian exile, was a reconstruction of the original and held deep historical and emotional significance. While it lacked the same opulence as its predecessor, the Second Temple remained a vital symbol of Jewish identity, unity, and connection to God.

The Second Temple era witnessed profound changes in religious practices and theological thought. It was during this time that synagogues, centers of study and prayer, gained prominence alongside the Temple. The Second Temple became a venue of spiritual renewal, where the Jewish people gathered for worship, study, and reflection.

Despite its importance, the Second Temple faced tumultuous times. It was defiled and desecrated by foreign forces, leading to a deep longing for its restoration. Tragically, the Second Temple was destroyed by the Romans in 70 CE, marking a significant turning point in Jewish history.

The Mishkan and the Temples symbolize the Jewish people's unwavering commitment to connecting with the Divine. They represent the spiritual centers where communal rituals, prayers, and sacrifices were offered as acts of devotion. The destruction of the Temples marked moments of sorrow and reflection, inspiring resilience and hope for the future.

While the physical structures of the Mishkan, First Temple, and Second Temple may no longer stand, their legacy endures. They serve as powerful reminders of the importance of worship, community, and the ongoing pursuit of a deeper relationship with God. Through the ages, Jews have found ways to adapt and evolve their religious practices, ensuring that the spirit of these sacred spaces continues to thrive in synagogues, homes, and hearts around the world.

The Second Temple in Jerusalem stood as a symbol of worship, connection, and devotion for the Jewish people. Among its sacred rituals, the sacrificial procession and the use of various types of incense held a significant place. These practices were integral to the spiritual life of the temple and were conducted with meticulous care and reverence.

The Sacrificial Procession: Central to the Second Temple's rituals was the offering of sacrifices. These offerings were seen as a means of communication between the people and the Divine, a way to seek forgiveness, express gratitude, or fulfill religious obligations. The sacrificial procession was a carefully choreographed ceremony involving various participants and stages.

Selection and Inspection: Animals designated for sacrifice were selected with utmost care. They were inspected for physical imperfections to ensure they met the rigorous standards of ritual purity. Only unblemished and healthy animals were deemed suitable for sacrifice.

Presentation & Laying on of Hands: The individual bringing the offering, often accompanied by a Cohen who, would present the animal at the designated area within the Temple courtyard

The person bringing the sacrifice would lay their hands on the head of the animal, symbolically transferring their intentions and prayers onto the offering. This act signified the connection between the worshiper and the Divine.

Butchering and Blood Collection: A staff of the both temples, were carefully picked who were professionally skilled in the proper method of butchering and other Holy tasks in Temples. The blood of the sacrificed animal was collected in a special vessel, and its subsequent application was an integral part of various rituals by the altar.

Altar Offering: Depending on the type of sacrifice, specific portions of the animal were placed on the altar. The remainder was distributed to Cohanim & Levites and in some sacrifices, the worshipers would receive a portion of the sacrificed animal, fostering a sense of communal participation.

Almighty's Art Gallery ©

Cohen HaGadol Offering
The 11 Sacred Incenses

Incense played a vital role in the worship within the Second Temple, particularly in the inner sanctum known as the Holy of Holies. The sacred incense was composed of a specific blend of eleven different ingredients, each carrying symbolic significance. The exact composition was known only to the priests entrusted with its preparation, and its use held great spiritual significance.

1. *Ingredients*: The eleven components of the sacred incense included stacte, onycha, galbanum, frankincense, myrrh, cassia, spikenard, saffron, costus, aromatic bark, and cinnamon. Each ingredient was carefully measured and combined to create a fragrant and spiritually potent mixture.

2. *Portions:* The exact number of different portions of each of these 11 incenses were gathered and mixed together once a year. The total would add up to 368 portions. Of which 365 portions were used daily half of the daily portion in the Morning services and the other half at the afternoon services. The remaining 3 portions were used in high holiday Yom Kippur by Cohen HaGadol, high priest.

3. *Preparation and Use*: The incense was prepared by grinding the various ingredients into a fine powder and blending them together. It was then placed on the golden altar of incense, which stood in the Holy Place just outside the Holy of Holies. Cohen HaGadol would enter the Holy of Holies once a year, on Yom Kippur, and offer the remainder 3 portions of incense before the Ark of the Covenant.

4. *Symbolism*: The sacred incense was imbued with deep symbolism. Its fragrant aroma was believed to represent the pleasing nature of the Jewish people's prayers rising to the Divine. The act of offering incense was a profound spiritual

experience, connecting the earthly realm with the heavenly.

The sacrificial procession and the use of sacred incense were integral components of the Second Temple's rituals, fostering a sense of awe, reverence, and connection to the Divine. These practices underscored the centrality of worship, the symbolism of offerings, and the belief in a direct relationship between human actions and the spiritual realm. The rituals of the Second Temple provided a framework for expressing faith, seeking forgiveness, and nurturing a deeper understanding of the mysteries of existence.

The Second Temples
Synagogues as Modern Temples
The Continuation of Sacred Spaces:

In the absence of the physical structures of the Mishkan and the Temples, synagogues have emerged as modern embodiments of sacred spaces, fulfilling the commandment of "וְעָשׂוּ לִי מִקְדָּשׁ וְשָׁכַנְתִּי

בְּתוֹכָם"*,"And You Shall make Me a Sanctuary, and I will Dwell Among Them" (Exodus 25:8).* Synagogues, much like their ancient counterparts, serve as centers of worship, learning, and community.

Synagogues: Houses of Prayer, Study, and Community Synagogues are not merely brick-and-mortar structures; they are sanctuaries where individuals gather to engage in prayer, study, and communal bonding. The sacredness of these spaces lies in their role as a meeting point between the divine and the human. When individuals enter a synagogue, they step into a realm where they can connect with G-Almighty through prayer, meditation and immerse themselves in the study of sacred texts, and engage in acts of kindness and charity.

A Place for Reflection and Connection Similar to the Mishkan and Temples, synagogues are places of introspection and self-discovery. They offer moments of solitude, meditation and reflection, allowing individuals to escape the distractions of the outside world and focus on their spiritual growth. In the serene atmosphere of a synagogue, people can connect with their inner selves, seek guidance, and find solace in the presence of the Divine.

Community Unity and Bonding Furthermore, synagogues serve as communal hubs where individuals from diverse backgrounds come together as one cohesive unit. Just as the Temples were places of pilgrimage and gathering of the Jewish people, Synagogues are spaces where the Jewish community congregates for celebrations, festivals, Shabbat services and shared experiences. This sense of unity strengthens the fabric of Jewish identity and fosters a sense of belonging and realizing you are not alone in your daily endeavors.

Many choose to perform some of the main commandments in synagogues, happy occasions such as circumcision, Bar Mitzvah, Wedding's Chupa or some other more somber occasions such as passing away of a person, or the process of remembering the person who has left us during the first year and annually.

Learning and Torah Study A significant aspect of synagogues is their role as centers of Torah study and intellectual growth. Just as the Tablets of the Law were housed in the Ark of the Covenant within the Temples, synagogues house Torah scrolls, the embodiment of Jewish wisdom and knowledge. Synagogue-based Torah study sessions and classes continue the tradition of delving into sacred texts, engaging in intellectual debates, and nourishing the mind and soul.

Holiness in Architecture, Bridging the Earth to Heavens
The Secret Sacred Role of Sanctuaries"

The echoes of the Mishkan and the Temples resound within these modern sanctuaries, reminding us that the pursuit of holiness, connection with the Divine, and communal unity remain timeless and enduring values at the heart of Judaism. Just as God's presence was felt within the Mishkan and the Temples of old, so too is His presence palpable within the walls of today's synagogues.

"And You shall make Me a sanctuary, and I will dwell among them" (Exodus 25:8) reflects a profound concept in the relationship between the Divine and humanity. At first the sentence does not make sense grammatically. The *apparent shift from singular to plural is not by mistake. Every letter written in Torah has a vast number of interpretations, but be sure, what is written and what you read are EXACT. This unusual shift from singular to plural is no exception and holds a significant theological and philosophical spiritual message.*

The initial instruction, "And they shall make Me **A** sanctuary," conveys the directive for the Israelites as One Nation to collectively construct a physical place of worship, the Mishkan (Tabernacle), as a dedicated space for Divine connection. This singular sanctuary symbolizes the unity and shared purpose of the entire community in creating A holy space for God's presence.

However, the subsequent part of the phrase, "and I will dwell amongst **THEM**, signifying a broader understanding. While the physical sanctuary is a singular structure, the Divine promise to dwell "among them" encompasses the entire community of Israel. *This plural aspect emphasizes thatGod's presence is not confined solely to the physical structure, but rather permeates the lives, actions, and collective spirit of the people.*

Of course, *let's not forget that many people say that I respect G-Almighty in my own way, in my own space, when I want, and how I want it*. Please let's look at the other side of the coin. Suppose you would like to discuss an important matter with a high-level person in your city or country. Would you still keep the same arguments? Meeting the King of Kings? No, Why?

Let's say, for the respect that G-Almighty deserves, you can assume it would be best if you schedule a meeting with his Omnipresence in his Holy sanctuary where he resides and not your backyard. That is assuming he would accept you. Of course, I am not suggesting that there is a problem with the backyard. No, the question becomes if you invite a high dignitary to your backyard, what would be the chance he will show up?

The interplay apposition of singular and plural serves to highlight the interplay between the tangible and the spiritual. The act of building the sanctuary is a communal effort, uniting the people in a shared endeavor to create a place of worship. However, the ultimate purpose of this sanctuary is to facilitate a deeper connection between God and the individual, as well as the community as a whole. The Divine promise to dwell "among them" underscores the idea that G-Almighty presence is not limited to a specific location but is accessible and manifest in the hearts, actions, and interactions of every individual within the community.

In essence, the verse encapsulates the concept that the sanctuary, while a physical construct, is a means to an end, fostering a spiritual connection and relationship between G-Almighty and His people. The shift from singular to plural captures the dynamic nature of this relationship, wherein the physical space serves as a conduit for a deeper, collective connection with the Divine. *The combination of singular and plural highlights the unity and diversity inherent in this sacred bond, reflecting the profound interplay between the individual and the community in their quest for spiritual elevation and closeness to God.*

Chapter 10

Jewish Ethical Living & Moral Values

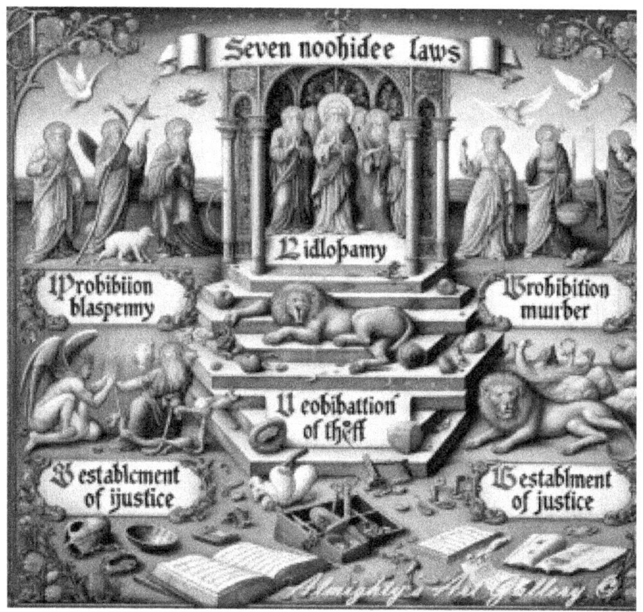

The Seven Noah Commandments – A MUST for Everyone

A non-Jew is bound ONLY by the 7 Noah's commandments passed by G-Almighty to Adam and Noah. Although this book is predominantly about the Jewish religion and cultures, I feel it is important to point out here these 7 essential commandments which gives everyone the framework for proper human behavior. As well as

G-Almighty's expects from us so that the humans can live together in

harmony.

1. NEVER slander NOR blasphemies your creator in gatherings and most importantly, not even in the privacy of your mind. Acknowledge in private and convey to others the knowledge of the existence of our ONE Creator who loves all of us, no matter what.
2. Never curse or swear to your creator. NEVER!!! (I beg to bring to your attention and warning; It is ONLY for your own good. Such as G-Damn)
3. Do NOT murder. Must I add??
4. Do NOT eat a limb or live animal. You eventually become what you eat!
5. Do NOT steal. Be happy with what you have, G-A so wished for you as such.
6. Refrain from incest, adultery, rape and homosexual relations. It is forbidden to make games with the natural human existence process.
7. Ensure Justice in the world; Establish court of laws.

Apersonal note to my dear, Non-Jewish Friends: As you can see, as a non-Jew, you are bound with only these 7 basic commandments. While a Jew is bound by 613 commandments. I am not sure if I have heard the expression of "***It is not easy to be a Jew***". I can vouch and affirm that it is not really easy, BUT I am happy and proud to be a Jew in the world we are living in, where Jews have outperformed in any field of thought and have always lit the torch of knowledge around the world of illiteracy. Considering the harsh history that Jews have experienced with so little manpower, so little natural resources and yet out-survived all the major emperors that had only one intention, Annihilate Jews!

But I MUST emphasize my greatest respect to the religion you comply or adhere to. We are ALL created by the same G-A. Although our beliefs might be different and disagree, our skin color varies, or our opinions diverge on different paths; We ALL have the same color blood running through our wonderfully created body, providing the proper nourishment to our amazing brain to function in exact precision that the best Rolex watch cannot imitate. We are brothers and sisters; We have the same ancestors in common. As a Jew, WE LOVE YOU, even if G-d forbid for some reason you decided otherwise.

Please do NOT trust just the(fake) news that the media tries to feed the viewer through different communication channels. I do not deny the existence of some of the horror videos you are exposed to. At the same time, I can tell you, on YouTube you can find so many professionally staged (disaster arena setup) artistically done scenes to show how terribly the Israeli Soldiers behave to the population!

Secrets of Judaism for a Long-Lasting Marriage Relationships

A successful and enduring marriage is a result of continuous effort, understanding, and commitment from both partners. While there is no one-size-fits-all formula for a lasting marriage, there are certain principles and practices that greatly contribute to a strong and harmonious Jewish relationship:

The Jewish community is often recognized for having relatively low divorce rates compared to other Western countries' demographics. While there can be variations within different Jewish communities, several factors contribute to the stability of marriage relationships among Jews. These factors align closely with the principles and practices and the commandments:

1. *Shared Values and Commitment*: Many Jewish marriages are rooted in a shared commitment to Jewish values, traditions, and religious practices. This shared foundation can provide a strong basis for couples to navigate challenges and work towards a harmonious relationship.

2. *Family and Community*: Jewish communities often emphasize the importance of family and community support. This network provides couples with a built-in system of encouragement, advice, and resources during times of difficulty. Jewish families often place a strong emphasis on family values, such as loyalty, mutual support, and commitment. These values can contribute to a stable and enduring marriage.

3. *Religious Practices:*Regular attendance at religious services, engagement in rituals, and participation in community events can foster a sense of belonging and connection. These practices often involve both partners, reinforcing their commitment to each other and their community.

4. *Communication and Conflict Resolution:* Many Jewish teachings emphasize the value of communication, empathy, and conflict resolution. Jewish couples may be more inclined to seek guidance from religious leaders or counselors who can provide them with tools for effective communication and problem-solving for a long-lasting quality relationship.

5. *Shared Rituals*: Celebrating Jewish holidays and observing rituals together can strengthen the emotional bond between partners. These shared experiences contribute to a sense of unity and connection in the relationship.

6. *Cultural and Historical Context:* The historical experiences of the Jewish people, including periods of persecution and diaspora, may have contributed to a sense of solidarity and the importance of maintaining strong familial bonds.

7. *Premarital Counseling:* In some Jewish communities, premarital counseling is thought and encouraged. This can provide couples with tools and insights to navigate challenges and strengthen their relationship from the outset as a couple prior to the Holy bondage of Marriage. The pre-marital relationships are prohibited and the extent to this prohibition is weighed by couples.

8. *Stigma of Divorce*: The stigma associated with divorce in some Jewish communities may deter couples from pursuing divorce without thoroughly exploring avenues for reconciliation and support.

9. *Religious Considerations*: In Orthodox Jewish communities, religious law and the process of obtaining a religious divorce (get) can add an additional layer of complexity to divorce proceedings, potentially leading couples to explore alternatives.

The Jewish community has one of the lowest divorce rates in the Western modern countries. This can be attributed to a combination of shared values, religious practices, family support, and a commitment to building and maintaining strong marriages. Upbringing the children as a couple. These factors create a supportive environment for couples to navigate challenges and work towards enduring relationships based on mutual understanding and respect.

Shabbat: Judaism's Gift to the World

Shabbat, the Jewish day of rest and spiritual rejuvenation, is a timeless gift that has been woven into the fabric of humanity by Judaism. This weekly day of joy, reflection, and connection has transcended cultural and religious boundaries, bringing its profound blessings to people around the world. The concept of Shabbat goes beyond religious observance; it encompasses a deep appreciation for rest, community, and the recognition of the sacred in everyday life.

At the heart of Shabbat is the idea of cessation. From Friday evening to Saturday evening, a sacred pause is taken from the hustle and bustle of daily mundane routines, work, and the demands of the outside world. This intentional pause offers a chance to step back, take a breath, and engage with life in a more mindful and meaningful way. It's a time to recalibrate, to charge your batteries, to slow down, and to connect with oneself, loved ones, and the Divine.

Shabbat is a time of joy. It's a day when families gather around the Shabbat table to share meals, stories, and blessings. The lighting of candles, the singing of songs, and the partaking of delicious food are all expressions of the joy that comes with Shabbat. The sense of unity and connection that permeates the Shabbat experience brings a unique kind of happiness that is deeply satisfying and fulfilling.

Rest is a fundamental aspect of Shabbat. It's not just physical rest, but a rest that encompasses the mind and soul. In a world that often prioritizes productivity and busyness, Shabbat reminds us of the importance of self-care and replenishment. By resting on Shabbat, we acknowledge our human limitations and embrace the need to recharge. This restfulness is a reminder that Jewish values are not solely determined by our achievements, but by the inherent worth of our existence.

Shabbat is a gift of time. In a culture that often rushes through life, Shabbat offers the opportunity to savor each moment. The absence of electronic devices, work-related activities, and other distractions allows us to be fully present. We engage in activities that nourish our souls, whether it's reading, conversing, taking leisurely walks, or simply enjoying nature's beauty. This precious gift of time enriches the Jewish lives by allowing focus on the things that truly matter.

The universal significance of Shabbat is evident in its impact on the world. Many cultures and religions have embraced the idea of a day of rest and reflection, influenced by the principles of Shabbat. The concept of a weekly pause has shown to be not only beneficial for individuals but also for societies at large. It has the potential to alleviate stress, strengthen family bonds, and promote overall well-being.

Shabbat reminds us of the importance of balance. In a world that often pulls us in various directions, Shabbat serves as an anchor. It teaches us that we are more than the sum of our achievements and that there is inherent value in simply being. This wisdom is a precious gift that Judaism has shared with humanity, fostering a deeper understanding of our shared human experience.

In essence, Shabbat is a day of rest, joy, and connection that transcends religious boundaries. It's a gift that offers us the opportunity to experience life in its fullest sense and to cultivate a sense of wonder, gratitude, and mindfulness. Through its universal principles, Shabbat continues to enrich the lives of people from all walks of life, inviting them to embrace the sacred rhythm of rest and renewal

Who is Rich?

As you might have noticed, this book is introducing you to the spiritual aspect of the Jewish life and belief. Of course, here is no exception.

Let's start with some basics. The attribute of modesty and content is so woven into every Jew by the last of the 10th commandment given to Moses on Mount Sinai over 3000 years ago:

(Exodus 20:17) "You shall not covet your neighbor's house; you shall not covet your neighbor's wife, or his male servant, or his female servant, or his ox, or his donkey, or anything that is your neighbor's."

It is forbidden to desire or lust after something that belongs to another person

This commandment brings home the understanding and realization in proportion to what we have is all given by G-A to us. He gives us possibly because of our good deeds or it is possible that we are being tested on how the person handles his belongings, and wealth. Does the person understand the players involved in his achievements? Does the person show compassion to his fellow beings by helping him and assisting the needy at the toughest times? Does the person see the G-Almighty as his partner? Did he set aside tenth of his income to charity?

Is the person content with all he has? Or always look at the neighbor's lawn to compare which is greener? One must realize what a person has at any point of his/her life is the best that G-A allotted for him and he must be modest, content and happy with all his belongings.

One must see the money and richness as a means for living and make the life better for others and not just for himself or his immediate family. One must not see the amount of the money he has as the measure of how much better or more successful a person he is than others.

Again, one should be thankful at all times to G-A to have made possible for the person's success and status in society.

Human nature is such and especially in our modern times that we get so arrogantly proud of our achievements or sometimes the illusion of accomplishments that we forget about our most important partner in life who has made it possible for us; G-A blessed be he.

The word RICH in Hebrew is עשיר.("Ashir") The four letters are the beginning of four body members, that would be the basics of being rich. as such:

Eyes Einaim ע עיניים

Teeth Shinaim ש שיניים

Hands Yadaim י ידיים

Feet Raglaim ר רגליים

So if you have been blessed with eyes, teeth, hands & feet, consider yourself as being RICH. Just think of it, if any of these are missing or impaired for some reason, what would one's life be like?

How would you like to test G-Almighty?
How would you like to be Rich? Ready to test the G-Almighty on the ONLY commandment which is allowed to us?

The attributes of compassion, kindness, charity=Tzedakah and mercy are shown and called upon humanity, knowing that not all are blessed equally for all kinds of known or unknown reasons. These attributes are highly prominent and notable in a Jewish life. The art of charity is so pronounced that every day in the morning prayer, there is a charity box that everybody gives to the welfare of the needy within or far from us. In addition, the Synagogues and learning institutions use the donations and annual fees for the upkeep, maintenance, salaries of Rabbanim, management and students. With the purpose of disseminate and propagate G-Almighty's existence and all his great attributes that he has bestowed upon us.

The children in their daily prayers are also accustomed and taught the habit of giving to charity, Tzedakah as well on a daily basis. By this act of giving, the person internalizes the feeling and emotions of another, up to even putting himself in the other's shoes hypothetically.

The idea of "Maaser" is an integrated.(system of giving the tenth of your income to the charity cause caring for the needy or can be a Jewish learning institution to spread the knowledge of G-Almighty to the world. *Keep the torch of knowledge lit onto the world.*

Humans are allowed in only one item to test the G-Almighty. The commandment of giving the tenth of your income is promised by G-A to be rewarded with so much wealth that would be immeasurable. By giving the tenth of your income, you have shown your loyalty, honesty, integrity, confidence and realization to perform commandments that do not even fit one's rational and logical mind. And Here is A promise to you:

Malachi (3:10). ***"Bring the whole tithe into the storehouse, that there may be food in my house. Test me in this," says The G-Almighty; And see if I will not open the floodgates of heaven and pour out so much blessing that you will not have enough room for it."***

Have you ever heard of any other promise as strong as this one! Of course, I would like to remind you this promise can be and certainly is a test of your maturity of all the attributes that one must absorb and digest spiritually as if looking into a mirror with G-Almighty's reflection.

So, if you dare to test the G-A, and I personally urge you to follow your instinct, just be on the outlook for your performance of at least some of these attributes: Compassion, Mercy, Kindness, Giving to Charity, Loyalty, Honesty, Integrity, Confidence, Sharing, Trustworthiness, Wholeness, and this is just to name a few.

Wishing you the BEST of all the good you wish for.

Chapter 11

Daily Devotions: Prayer and Reflection, The Soul Adhesive

Daily Prayers (AM, Noon, PM)
What is prayer? Why do we pray? Who do we really pray for?

Prayer is a religious duty, an integral part of Jewish life in the process

of appreciating our existence and being. There are many laws and

traditions around prayers.

The prayer is a way for a person to connect to his creator to have a quality time. "Just two of US." Think of it as the person's opportunity to meet the King of the Kings, for pouring his heart to the one who listens patiently, reads one's thoughts, and requests. The one who knows everything, thoughts, imaginations, inside & out. And you know what? I do not know of anyone who tried to reach the G-Almighty and was refused. Consider this scenario, try scheduling a face-to-face meeting with your Mayor, Senator, VP, or the President. What are the chances of an immediate meeting? any time? place of your choice? Just to make this clear, you can have a meeting with G-Almighty when you choose in your heart. Although the stature and prominence of the Omnipresence should not be forgotten. For such a grandiose meeting, the person must be dressed properly, with a clear mind to join the prayers with the congregation for the proper acceptance of his splendor.

When the Glory of Temples (1st&2nd) were present, sacrifice offerings were part of daily routines. The sacrifice of the tame animal was as part of a person's repentance of his sins, giving thanks to G-Almighty or performing his duty as part of his 613 commandments.

Since the holy temples were destroyed, the sacrifice offering has been replaced by the prayers that were composed by the 120 Sages of the Great Assembly. Performing some of the commandments are impossible due to the fact they have to be performed in the Temple premises.

Notwithstanding a Jew's constant acknowledgment of G-Almighty in every imaginable facet of life throughout the day, from the time he opens his eyes with uttering "Modeh Ani= Giving Thanks to our creator to have returned our soul back to us" or constant prayers and blessings said on cleansing, eating, drinking (before & after), smelling, and so much more, There are formal collective prayers scheduled for all during the various times in day. Morning, usually prior to starting a day, Mid-day afternoon prayers, usually from noon to prior to sunset, and finally at night, after the sunset to about half hour before sunrise next day. Of course, these are formal prayers. Beyond the individual responsibility of the prayers one can spend his time wisely by learning Torah, Talmud, or reading the chapters or the whole book of Psalm on a regular basis.

As part of transition preparation from being awake to sleep mode, where our soul leaves us (temporary majority of the time), there is a prayer before bed which we prepare our soul to take a daily report to G-Almighty on all our deeds during the day

All in all, you can find an observant Jew, who spends at least 2 to many more hours in a day in prayers to blessings. And this is not including the prayers of Shabbat or Holidays that the minimum is a lot longer than 2 hours.

Most are structured best to pray in congregation as it requires a quorum minimum of 10 men (age over Bar Mitzvah 13 years old). Each of prayers were instituted by our Patriarchs, forefathers: (**AM**: Avraham; **Noon**: Isaac; **Night**: Jacob)

Prayers are recited from the structured books called Siddur. A Chazan or Cantor takes lead in the reading of the prayers out loud. His role is considered as a defense attorney, who will, with his prayers representing all present, bring our shortcomings and sins to the attention of the Holy one and still request for forgiveness, health, wealth for all. Chazan's humility, humbleness, charisma, presentation, voice, clarity of expression through the prayers are highly considered in selecting the cantor. It is customary to invite the person who has "Chiuv"=Obligation, (a person whose immediate relative has passed away for the period of one year, or remembering those relatives who have left us on the annual passing date.)

The Role of Siddur in Judaism

The oldest printed prayer book (siddur) known is the "Seder Roma" (Rome Prayer Book). It was printed in Rome, Italy, on the eve of Rosh Hashanah in 1486 by a Jewish printer named Abraham Isaac Conat.

This siddur follows the Sephardic prayer tradition and includes both daily prayers and Yom Kippur prayers.

The "Seder Roma" is one of the earliest printed siddurim and holds historical significance. It features artistic elements and meticulous printing, making it an important artistic creation of its time.

Although it is attributed to Rabbi Amshel of France, its excessive errors and amendments suggest that he may have been working on it, at least in its earliest version, at the time it was printed.

This siddur is part of a historical exhibit, displayed in the Synagogue Syndicate Building in Jerusalem in October 2009, alongside other early printed prayer books from the beginnings of Hebrew printing in the Land of Israel.

A Spiritual Meditation Journey Through Prayer

Some consider a meditation phase by listening to the Chazan's prayers as such an uplifting spiritual experience. By Chazan's absolute clear thought of his awesome responsibility of the moment, to have a one-to-one conversation with G-Almighty on behalf of everyone present in the congregation. Imagine the opportune time: While the Cantor is praying, the person closes his eyes, by deep meditation to perceive the sensation that *it is HE himself* who is having this extra-terrestrial experience. Think of it; Encounter with Glorious G-Almighty, "King of Kings". At least 3 times a day!

And yet there are those who by their level of intentions of the prayer have a more structured platform to contemplate reflection with His Omnipresence. As part of the structured portions of Siddur and its contents, for the morning prayer, Shacharit, which usually takes between 45 minutes to as long as hours. There are four major portions that are directly associated with the spiritual realm of prayer and the connection of the Soul to the splendor and brilliance of the Majestic Omnipresent. The closeness that one would feel through his prayers depends on the intentions, internalizing with the understanding of the words one reads through Siddur. The depth of the intentions that one invests in reciting the prayer, indicates the level of spirituality that he strives to attach himself to G-Almighty. Below are the levels of connections and closing to minimum proximity with magnificent radiations of G-Almighty.

1. *The World of Creation (Yetzirah):* This is the first part of the prayer, and it is meant for blessings and praises to express the significance and beauty of Almighty's creation. The person acknowledges the importance and beauty of the world and expresses gratitude for it.

2. *The World of Formation (Asiyah):* The next section, Pesukei Dezimra, acknowledges the organized and structured world and prepares his soul for a spiritual encounter with G-

Almighty. This section sets the stage for the central part of the prayer.

3. **_The World of Action (Atzilut)_:** "Shema Israel is the predominant prayer included in this phase of exhilarating uplifting. The person focuses his meditation on the unity with the Omnipresent and the love and devotion one should have for Him. The blessings emphasize his Majesty's creative power and our obligation to love Him and follow His commandments.

4. **_The World of Emanation (Beriyah)_:** During the Amidah=standing, the person ascends to a higher spiritual realm and engages in intimate dialogue with G-Almighty on a one-to-one basis. The Amidah consists of 19 blessings that cover various aspects of life, and it is a time for personal reflection, confession, and making specific requests.

All prayers continue with further reciting chapters from Psalms, Mishnah, which can be co-compared with trying to calm down after such an extraordinary liaison with His Majesty and concludes with finale Aleinu LeShabeach.

These different realms in the morning prayer service help guide the worshiper through a spiritual journey, beginning with praise and gratitude, reaffirming faith, and culminating in a personal and intimate connection with Almighty. Each section serves a unique purpose in the worshiper's encounter with the Divine.

In addition to daily prayers, there are special Prayers for Shabbat, new month, new year, holidays, fast days. Usually on these special days, we take out the Sefer Torah and read special portions related to the occasion.

Mincha, & Arvit/Maariv (afternoon & night) prayers can take from 20 minutes to half an hour, while the Morning Shacharit takes about 45 minutes to 2 or more hours on Shabbat and even more on high holidays. Yom Kippur is considered as the Judgment Day and every effort is made to get closer to the Almighty and request forgiveness for all the sins that we have sinned (by knowing or not knowing) during the past year. This closeness is acquired by structured prayers in his Holy residence, "The Synagogues" in void of Holy Temples. Yom Kippur's prayers can take up a major portion of the 25 hours day holiday.

There are various formats of the siddurim for Ashkenazi, Sephardi, Chabad, and Chasidi. Specially made versions of Siddurim are available for the children to acquaint the young from the early stages of childhood to the rich culture & traditions of Judaism while planting the seeds of faith & confidence to Majesty of King of the Kings. There are special Siddurim for the daughters & women with added portions of Psalms for the Segula=Virtues for different requests from Almighty, such as health, wealth, request for children, or finding the proper match for the children (Just to name a few).

Shema Israel: The Heart of Jewish Faith

"Shema Israel" is arguably the most famous words in Jewish prayer, encapsulating the core of Jewish monotheism and spirituality. This short but profound phrase holds deep meaning and significance within Jewish tradition, serving as a unifying declaration of faith and a daily reminder of G-Almighty's presence in the life of every Jew.

The phrase "Shema Israel" is derived from the Book of Deuteronomy 6:4, which reads, " =‏"שמע ישראל ה' אלוקינו ה' אחד"*Hear, O Israel: The Lord our G-Almighty, the Lord is one.*" These words are recited three times daily by observant Jews, in the morning/(Shacharit), evening/(Arvit or Maariv), & before going to bed. The complete portions of Shema takes about 3 minutes to read by an average reader.At its essence, the Shema is a declaration of the monotheistic faith at the heart of Judaism, the belief in the absolute oneness of G-Almighty.

It is a proclamation of His uniqueness, His existence & excellence as the sole Creator and Ruler of the universe. For a Jew, it is a profound expression of devotion, a declaration of his loyalty to G-Almighty.

Beyond its theological significance, the Shema also carries a practical and ethical message. Following the opening declaration, the Shema continues with a call to love G-Almighty with all one's heart, soul, and might and to teach these commandments diligently to one's children. This emphasizes the central role of education and ethical living in Jewish life. *The codes of ethics of proper living and behavior to others as etched in the Holy Torah, are etched on the memory genes of every Jew.*

The Shema is not just a recitation; it's a call to action. It serves as a daily reminder to live a life that reflects G-Almighty's teachings and values. Jews are encouraged to internalize these words, letting them guide their actions, decisions, and interactions with others.

Moreover, the Shema is a unifying force in Judaism, connecting Jews across time and space. Regardless of individual backgrounds, practices, or denominations, Jews worldwide recite these words, reinforcing a shared heritage and commitment to G-Almighty.

"Shema Israel" is more than a simple prayer; it's a declaration of faith, a commitment to living ethically, and a bond that unites Jews across the globe. It serves as a constant reminder that monotheism, ethical living, and a deep connection to G-Almighty are at the heart of Jewish identity and spirituality.

We are reminded to shine the light of the knowledge by the ethical value codes of the 10 commandments given to Jews at Mount Sinai and the 613 commandments passed to us by Moshe and our great sages, known as "Torah Baal Peh"="Torah By-Heart/Memory"

The Profound Essence of Tefilah: A Comprehensive Exploration

Tefilah, the act of Jewish prayer, stands at the heart of Jewish spirituality and serves as a profound connection between humans and the Divine. Rooted in ancient traditions and evolving over centuries,

Tefilla encompasses a wide range of prayers, each carrying its own significance, structure, and purpose. From daily prayers to special occasions like the High Holidays of Rosh Hashanah and Yom Kippur, Tefilah provides a means of communication, reflection, and spiritual growth.

The daily prayers, also known as the Amidah or ShemonehEsrei, constitute a central part of Jewish prayer. Comprising 19 blessings, these prayers cover various themes, including praise, gratitude, requests, and supplication. Structured around the themes of Avot (ancestors), Gevurot (powers), Kedushat Hashem (holiness of Almighty), and more, the Amidah allows individuals to connect with the Divine on a personal and collective level. These prayers are generally recited silently, allowing for introspection and deep contemplation.

The High Holidays, including Rosh Hashanah and Yom Kippur, mark a profound period of introspection, repentance, and renewal in the Jewish calendar. The prayers during these holidays emphasize themes of self-examination, accountability, and forgiveness. The Rosh Hashanah and Yom Kippur prayers powerfully reflects the idea of Divine judgment and the fragility of human life. Through the sounding of the shofar. Tefilah during the High Holidays is intensified by internalizing the awe, inspiration, reflection, and commitment to Almighty.

Rosh Hashanah and Yom Kippur Prayers

The Jewish New Year, and the Day of Atonement, stand as the holiest days in the Jewish calendar. The Tefilah on Rosh Hashanah emphasizes themes of renewal, kingship of G-Almighty, and his covenant with Jewish people. The Tefilah on Yom Kippur, on the other hand, centers on repentance, confession, and seeking forgiveness. The Kol Nidre prayer, recited at the beginning of Yom Kippur, symbolizes the earnest desire for a clean slate and starting anew.

Tefilah engages multiple senses, creating a multisensory experience that deepens the connection between the individual and the Divine.

The tactile sensation of holding a prayer book or touching the mezuzah as one enters a prayer space serves as a physical reminder of one's spiritual intention. The auditory experience of reciting prayers, chanting melodies, and listening to the shofar's sounds during the High Holidays enhances the emotional impact of Tefilah. Additionally, the visual elements of prayer, including the placement of the Ark where the Torah's are stored with utter respect, and the use of prayer shawls (Tallit), contribute to a holistic experience that engages mind, body, and soul.

Purpose of Tefillah: Tefilah serves a myriad of purposes within the Jewish tradition. It provides a structured means of expressing gratitude, seeking guidance, and connecting with the Divine. Tefilah also serves as a channel for self-reflection, encouraging individuals to examine their actions, intentions, and moral compass. Furthermore, Tefilah fosters a sense of community, as individuals join together in congressional prayer, sharing in a collective experience of spiritual devotion.

Tefilah, in its diverse forms, encapsulates the essence of Jewish spirituality and values. From daily prayers that offer a consistent connection with the Divine to the profound Tefilah of the High Holidays that inspire introspection and transformation, the act of Jewish prayer serves as a vehicle for communication, reflection, and growth. Its multifaceted nature engages the senses, emotions, and intellect, creating a holistic experience that binds individuals to their heritage and strengthens their connection to Almighty and community.

Aleinu LeShabeach: The Grand Finale of Every Jewish Prayer

In the tapestry of Jewish ritual services, the "Aleinu LeShabeach" prayer stands out as a powerful and emotional heart-rending conclusion to each of the daily prayer services. Its placement at the end of the prayers is not merely coincidental; rather, it serves as a climax of the spiritual journey that one embarks upon during prayer. The Aleinu encapsulates the essence of Jewish faith, hope, and mission, and its recitation serves as a reminder of the unique relationship between God and the Jewish people.

The opening lines of the Aleinu, which translate to "It is our duty to praise the Master of all," immediately set the tone for the prayer. These words emphasize the Jewish people's obligation to recognize and extol the oneness of Almighty. This acknowledgment is not just a passive affirmation but a call to action. By declaring G-Almighty's singularity, Jews are also committing to the responsibilities that come with being chosen nation.The Aleinu goes on to contrast the worship of Almighty with the idolatrous practices of other nations.

This distinction serves as a constant reminder of the Jewish people's unique role in the world, to be a light unto other nations and to guide humanity towards the recognition of one true God. The prayer does not aim to belittle other faiths but rather to emphasize the Jewish mission of monotheistic advocacy.

Perhaps the most stirring part of the Aleinu is its vision of the future, a time when "all the inhabitants of the world will come to recognize as G-Almighty is only ONE and every knee would bend to His Majesty." This messianic hope is not just a dream of global monotheism but also a yearning for a world united in peace, understanding, and divine recognition. The Aleinu's finale is a call for the establishment of Almighty's kingdom on Earth, a time when his Majestic presence will be universally acknowledged and celebrated by all the nations of the world.

Aleinu, provides the worshippers with a moment of reflection and aspiration. After traversing the highs and lows of personal and communal prayers, the Aleinu offers a vision of a perfected world. It serves as a reminder that prayer is not just a personal endeavor but is intrinsically linked to the broader mission of the Jewish people as Am Echad=One Nation.

In essence, the Aleinu LeShabeach is not just a prayer but a declaration of faith, a roadmap for the Jewish mission, and a beacon of hope for the future. Its position as the finale of each prayer service ensures that worshippers leave with a renewed sense of purpose, inspired to transform the world in line with the lofty ideals of the commandments which it embraces.

Chapter 12

Conclusions

***Embracing the Multifaceted Jewish Identity: A Comprehensive
Exploration of Attributes***

I have had the pleasure of meeting various friends from all over the

world. In my many chats with the fiends and tourists who visit or

planning to visit Israel, I noticed how limited the knowledge and

understanding of the non-Jews and some Jews who visit this great land

called "The Holy Land" and the people who make up this tiny land, the

Jews.

I thought to myself, based on our belief, we the Jews have the responsibility of being the light to the Nations of the World. Further, I noticed how much in our daily/holiday prayers & book of the Psalms, we pray and include the Nations of the World.

I noticed that most of the basic information available to a novice reader is through TV or social media, which are at least 80% fake news. Other sources of the information are usually through the Sunday bible classes, which are explained in the most basic way and most are often forgotten and events of the Torah are vaguely remembered from the early ages of studying the bible. Other sources of information on Jewish sources are either so complex or the person does not even know what questions to ask or where to look for the honest down to earth simple question on Judaism.

I believe this lack of the information is the root to the widespread Anti-Semitism throughout the turbulent history the Jewish people experienced up to the current days where Anti-Semitism which is sprouting like mushrooms in every corner of the world-even in Israel. Jews almost constantly, had and still have to hide or forfeit their pride in Judaism, while hiding their identity to avoid prosecutions & senseless and rootless killings and annihilation attempts on Jews no matter where in the world.

With these in mind, I embarked on the journey to pass what I have learned to others (commandment) to enlighten those seeking to decipher Judaism. When I started to expand on the idea I wrote 10-15 of the most basics of Judaism as a religion and culture. Soon I found myself in never ending subjects that sprouted that characterizes the person as a Jew. Each subject would direct me to another few subjects that I had to include in this book clarifying or further explanation. The goal of keeping the book as simplistic as possible and still under 100 pages were long forgotten by the vast amount of information that I had to bring to light to a minimum of explaining Judaism-Even for a glimpse.

I challenged myself that this book must bring a new angle of vision on Judaism while it should be as comprehensive as possible. In my search I came to realize the spiritual aspect of Jewish living and traditions are so mysterious and misunderstood. Of course, I am sure you agree with the complexity of the task to explain something that you cannot see or touch. Explanation of the inner secrets of spirituality of Jewish culture, religion and traditions that is so interwoven in the genes of every Jew throughout history.

While this book has outrun my original purpose and expectations, my sincere hope is that this book will serve as a tool fighting the Anti-Semitism in the world.

The conclusion of any book serves as the culminating chapter, bringing together the myriad themes, ideas, and concepts discussed throughout the narrative. In the context of exploring the diverse attributes that collectively constitute a person's Jewish identity, the conclusion serves as a final canvas upon which the rich tapestry of Jewish spiritual heritage, history, religion, culture, and values is woven. Through an exploration of various aspects such as faith, history, tradition, culture, and connection to the land, this essay seeks to encapsulate the essence of Jewish faith, a sentiment that transcends geographical boundaries and generations.

Faith and Spirituality:

Central to the Jewish identity is faith, which has remained unwavering across generations despite the challenges faced by the community. Judaism is a fabric of beliefs, traditions, and rituals that span from biblical times to the modern era. The Jewish faith, rooted in monotheism, offers a unique perspective on spirituality and the relationship between humanity and the Divine, G-Almighty. The centrality of practices such as prayer, study of sacred texts, and observance of commandments underscores the depth of Jewish spirituality. The conclusion brings to light the resiliency of Jewish faith in the face of adversity and the profound impact it has had on shaping individuals and communities.

Historical Resonance:

Jewish history demonstrates the threads of triumph and tragedy, resilience and perseverance. From ancient times to the Holocaust and beyond, the conclusion underscores the importance of acknowledging and understanding the historical events that have shaped the Jewish identity. The horrors of the Holocaust serve as a stark reminder of the consequences of unchecked hatred and discrimination. Conversely, the narrative of Jewish contributions to civilization, through scholarship, art, science, and more paint a picture of an identity of a small nation who has assisted the Nations of the World in every avenue of human society & progress.

Imagine a forest where unfortunately the anger of fire savagely ravaged it totally, but the next year with the change of weather and the rainfalls a new branch slowly and surely stands tall over all the burnt trees. This in short explains Judaism and the State of Israel.

Cultural Diversity:

The Jewish identity is a mosaic of cultures that have evolved across a multitude of regions and historical contexts. From the Ashkenazi Jews of Eastern Europe to the Sephardic Jews of the Iberian Peninsula or the Ethiopian Jews who were mass emigrated to Israel in Operation Shlomo and beyond, the conclusion celebrates the richness of cultural diversity within Judaism. The various seemingly dissimilar of local languages, yet the unique Jewish language, traditions, cuisines, and customs that bond the Jews anywhere in the world, is a testament to the adaptability, resiliency and dynamism of Jewish culture.

Connection to Israel:

The significance of Israel in the Jewish identity cannot be overstated. The conclusion highlights the powerful bond that Jews around the world share with the land of Israel, a connection that transcends time and distance. The return to the land, the establishment of the modern state of Israel, and the ongoing struggles and triumphs resonate deeply with Jews across the globe, reinforcing the notion of a shared heritage and destiny.

Ethical Values:

Judaism is built on a foundation of ethical values that emphasize justice, compassion, and the pursuit of righteousness. The conclusion delves into the concept of Tikkun Olam, the Jewish principle of repairing the world through acts of kindness and social responsibility based on the Almighty's commandments. From charitable acts to the pursuit of social justice, these values form an integral part of the Jewish identity, reflecting a commitment to making the world a better place to live, for everyone!.

The attributes that constitute a person's Jewish identity are multifaceted and interconnected, creating a portrait that is as complex as it is profound. This exploration has delved into the intricate layers of faith, history, culture, connection to Israel, and ethical values that collectively define the essence of being Jewish. This identity is not confined to the pages of history; rather, it is a living tapestry that continues to evolve, adapt, and inspire. At the conclusion of this journey, we are reminded that being Jewish is more than a label, it is a mosaic of experiences, beliefs, and values that enrich the individual and contribute to the diversity of the global human experience.

Writer's Challenge to our Dear Reader
Embracing Ethical Living

In a world filled with diverse beliefs and ideologies, the pursuit of ethical living remains a common thread that binds humanity together. As a writer, it is my privilege to extend a challenge to our dear readers. A challenge that transcends religious boundaries and cultural differences. This challenge revolves around embracing the principles of ethical conduct by aligning with the seven Noahite's commandments and unofficially adopting some of the values & traits a Jewish is bound to in day-to-day lives. By doing so, we not only contribute to our personal growth but also foster a more harmonious and compassionate world.

The seven Noahide's laws provide a foundation for moral conduct that can resonate with people of various faiths and beliefs. These principles include refraining from idolatry, blasphemy, murder, theft, illicit relations, cruelty to animals, and establishing a just legal system. These commandments are a universal call to uphold the sanctity of life, respect for others, and the creation of a just and compassionate society. By committing to following these ethical guidelines, we contribute to the well-being of our communities and demonstrate our shared commitment to upholding basic human dignity.

By unofficially embracing some of the Jewish values and ethical principles that guide day-to-day living, such as kindness (chesed), compassion (Rachamim), truth & honesty (Emet), humility (Anavah), and gratitude (HakaratHatov) exemplify the commitment to ethical conduct. Incorporating these values into our lives enriches our interactions, fosters empathy, and nurtures a sense of interconnectedness. By practicing kindness and compassion, we cultivate an environment of understanding and unity that transcends differences.

The Challenge:

Dear reader, I would like to challenge you to embark on a journey of ethical living by adhering to the seven Noahite's commandments and embracing some of the virtues embodied in Jewish values. Imagine the impact of such a commitment on your daily interactions, decisions, and relationships. Challenge yourself to refrain from actions that harm others, to foster understanding and respect, and to promote justice and compassion.

For Men: You are walking in the street, and a foxy lady (& I mean FOX), passes by you. She does not belong to you, STOP looking at her right away (no more than a couple of seconds). Show that you are content with the beautiful wife G-Almighty has given to you. As he wants the best for you.

For Women: G-Almighty has created you as the most beautiful person ever. Exercise modesty and chastity; You do not need to expose parts of your body to others to grab their attention. Your body is yours only and you can share ONLY with whom you decide, not everyone else.

As you navigate this challenge or any other challenge you might embrace for yourself, remember that ethical living is not a solitary pursuit but a collective endeavor. By adopting these principles, you contribute to the betterment of yourself and the society as a whole, fostering an environment where people of all backgrounds can coexist harmoniously. Imagine the ripple effect your actions can create, a wave of positive change that touches lives far beyond your immediate circle.

In a world that often seems so fragmented, embracing ethical living offers a unifying path. This challenge is not about religious conversion, but about making a conscious choice to be an agent of positive change. By adhering to these principles, we contribute to the creation of a world marked by respect, empathy, and justice. your actions & behavior become a beacon of light that guides others towards a more ethical and compassionate existence. So please pass it on.

In conclusion, I would like you to leave you with the prayer: May G-Almighty bless you in all your positive wishes, shine his light on you and your path and all your loved ones. Wish you the best of everything you wish for yourself or your loved ones.

Humbly presented,

Isaac Pirian.

Your comments & opinions are most welcomed: